*Academic Leadership
in Community Colleges*

Published by the University of Nebraska Press for
The Center for the Study of Higher and Postsecondary Education
Department of Educational Administration
Teachers College
University of Nebraska–Lincoln

Academic Leadership
in Community Colleges

Alan T. Seagren
Daniel W. Wheeler
John W. Creswell
Michael T. Miller
Kimberly VanHorn-Grassmeyer

University of Nebraska Press
Lincoln and London

The paper in this book meets the minimum requirements of
American National Standard for Information Sciences—Permanence
of Paper for Printed Library Materials, ANSI Z39.48-1984.

Library of Congress Cataloging-in-Publication Data

Academic leadership in community colleges/edited by

Alan T. Seagren . . . [et al.]. p.   cm.

Includes bibliographical references.

ISBN 0-8032-4242-5

1. Community colleges – United States – Administration.

2. Departmental chairmen (Universities and colleges) – United States.

I. Seagren, Alan T., 1932– .   II. University of Nebraska – Lincoln.

Center for the Study of Higher and Postsecondary Education.

LB2341.A227 1994 378.1'00973 – dc20

93-31026 CIP

CONTENTS

Community/Technical College presidents, vice presidents, and deans come primarily from the ranks of faculty. Many gain administrative experience serving as department or division chairs. Although the chair position is widely regarded as key to the effective functioning of a college's major academic and career programs, those filling the positions generally receive little or no formal preparation for the job.

Over the past decade leadership development has been designed for Community/Technical College presidents, vice presidents, and deans to prepare them for their new responsibilities. Few, if any, opportunities have been available for Community/Technical College chairs, who outnumber all other types of administrators combined. The individual assuming the role of a department or division chair is quite often under-prepared, overworked, and undertrained. Unlike the private sector, which devotes considerable dollars to training on-line supervisors, Community/Technical Colleges have provided limited support for their mid-level academic leaders.

Reports in the literature and inputs from a range of Community/Technical College systems and institutions indicate that there is a growing level of concern about the identification, selection, and preparation of individuals to assume academic leadership positions as they become available. Maricopa Community Colleges, Phoenix, Arizona, identified approximately 12,500 academic leaders (deans and chairs) from over 1,500 Community/Technical Colleges located in the United States and Canada. Projections indicate about 40% of these current administrators will retire by the year 2000. Thus, approximately 5,000 individuals will need to be recruited and trained over the next six years to replace current administrators.

The National Community College Chair Academy (NCCCA) was created to respond to this leadership training need. The idea of the NCCCA and the programs and services offered through them have been a direct result of a grass roots movement by chairs within the Maricopa Community Colleges. The primary mission and focus of the NCCCA is to "Advance Academic Leadership" for chairs, deans, and other instructional leaders. To achieve this mission, the NCCCA offers a number of services focusing on leadership: Annual conferences; Institutes for Academic Leadership Development; Information resources (i.e., ChairNET, an on-line electronic information network, databases/bibliographies developed in conjunction with ERIC, and a speaker's bureau); Publications, including the NCCCA scholarly journal *Academic Leadership*; and cutting edge research activities.

The NCCCA developed a partnership with the Center for the Study of Higher and Postsecondary Education (CSHPE) at the University of Nebraska-Lincoln to conduct research and develop much needed academic leadership development programs. One of the first research activities undertaken by the CSHPE in conjunction with the NCCCA was to develop a comprehensive survey, which was distributed to 9,000 Community/Technical College chairs in the U.S. and Canada. Approximately 3,000 chairs returned the survey.

Academic Leadership in Community Colleges was developed from the data obtained from this study. The effort has resulted in a dual benefit to those of us who endeavor to improve and expand leadership preparation for chairs, deans, and other instructional leaders within Community/Technical Colleges. The book is a valuable resource for individuals designing professional development programs focusing on leadership. Of equal importance, *Academic Leadership in Community Colleges* should help the leaders within Community/Technical Colleges be more responsive to the academic, occupational, and technical needs of students and the training needs of business and industry. I hope you agree.

> Dr. Gary Filan
> Executive Director
> National Community College Chair Academy

The community college chair is like a juggler who initiates, controls, and halts the objects being juggled. These objects may be competing priorities, interests, agendas, and expectations. The juggling act is made more difficult in that these objects are seen differently by individuals and groups—faculty, students, senior administrators, businesses and industry, and the community at large. Any true "leader" in the community college cannot afford to let the objects fall to the floor, or ignore them in the air. Moreover, it is the hands of a chair that keep the objects in the air - the chair effectively spans the gaps among the competing groups both on and off campus. And the chair is in the middle, feeling the pressures of the objects in flight, delicately balancing interests, and hoping that the final act will receive a standing ovation.

This book reports the first study of chairpersons in community colleges. The study provides insight into four major components of chairs' professional lives (personal characteristics, responsibilities, challenges, and strategies), and is intended to emphasize the importance of professional development of chairs. The study has two specific purposes. First, to develop a data base about pressing academic leadership development needs which can be the focus of conferences, workshops, and the Institute for Academic Leadership Development activities offered by the National Community College Chair Academy. Second, to provide individuals holding the chair position with information about the importance of working with faculty, serving students, visioning, dealing with change, and responding to business and community interests.

The data base is comprehensive. Responses were received from approximately 3000 academic leaders (deans and chairs/heads) in community colleges across the United States and Canada. Much of the meaningful research completed in recent years has focused primarily on the chair role in four-year institutions. Although the missions and structure of four-year institutions differ from these of two-year institutions, the role of the chair in both types of institutions is similar in many respects. Chairs often assume their positions with little training, and after acquiring the post, feel caught in the middle between the competing pressures of faculty expectations and mandates from upper administration. Previous studies were helpful in developing the survey instrument for chairs in two-year institutions. This project both modifies and expands the literature for the unique mission of community colleges.

This book is organized into three sections. **PART I: Overview and Profile of Academic Leaders, Their Instructional Units and Their Campuses.** In Chapter One an introduction to the study is presented. A profile of the chairs is described in Chapter Two. In Chapter Three the characteristics of both instructional units and campuses in which chairs work are described.

PART II: Chair Perceptions and Job Dimensions. This section is a discussion of chair responses to six job dimensions: educational beliefs and values, roles, tasks, skills, challenges, and strategies. The responses tell us what philosophical perspectives guide the chairs' work and the importance they ascribe to varied aspects of their work. Each chapter includes a section outlining implications of the findings for leadership development, and institutional policy and structure. Chapter Four describes chair attitudes toward select educational beliefs and values. Chapters Five, Six and Seven include chair perceptions of the importance of specific roles, tasks and skills for their everyday work. Chapters Eight and Nine report both the challenges chairs perceive as impacting or impeding their work, and specific strategies in response to these challenges. The final chapter in this section, Chapter Ten, provides insights into the potential impact of selected institutional and personal characteristics on beliefs and values, roles, tasks, skills, challenges, and strategies.

PART III: Summary and Reflections. Chapter Eleven presents a summary of the study findings by profiling the characteristics of a "typical" chair and identifies the need for future study of leadership issues.

It is our hope that readers will see something of themselves in these pages. We believe that academic leaders will feel empowered with the recognition that their beliefs, and the manner in which they approach their jobs, have been highlighted and are shared by others. In addition, we hope that chairs will be challenged to look to the views of their peers, and consider incorporating some new ways of reflecting upon and acting in their professional lives. Finally, the results of the study have influenced topics included in the Institute for Academic Leadership Development and the International Conference for Community College Chairs, Deans and Other Instructional Leaders conducted by the National Community College Chair Academy.

ACKNOWLEDGMENTS

To the many individuals involved in the preparation of this book, we are deeply indebted. Especially we would like to give credit to Dr. Gary L. Filan, Executive Director, National Community College Chair Academy, who gave generously of his time, provided continued support, insightful review and funding for the project. A special thanks is also given to the NCCCA staff for compiling the list of chairs, distributing the survey and tabulating the data, and to the participants from the first (1992) NCCCA Institute for Academic Leadership Development who completed the pilot administration of the survey, and provided helpful comments and critique.

Gratitude is expressed to the staff of the Center for the Study of Higher and Postsecondary Education at UN-L who provided valuable direction in the planning stage of the project and the development of the survey. Center staff included Lindsay Barker, Rich Bringelson, Bob Brown, Leon Cantrell, Ron Joekel, Mac Sawyer, and Delivee Wright. Lindsay Barker is deserving of special recognition for his contribution to the conceptualization of the model of the Department Chair which provided direction for development of the survey. The following individuals are recognized for helpful review and critique at various phases of the project: Robert Eicher, LaVerne Franzen, Jack Huck, Barry Lumsden, Robin Menschenfruend, David Pierce, and Ken Robson.

An Executive Summary of the material in this manuscript was presented at the Second Annual International Conference for Community College Chairs, Deans, and Other Instructional Leaders. In addition, portions of the material have been used in regional and national workshops; thus, we are indebted to hundreds of individuals who have reviewed, reacted, and helped to clarify the ideas.

Finally, special thanks are extended to Cheryl Ross, who prepared varied materials throughout the project; to Diane Greenlee, who provided technical editing assistance; to Han Hua Wang who provided research assistance; and to Christy Harnden, Cindy DeRyke, and the other members of the Word Processing Center and Instructional Design Center in Teachers College at UN-L for preparing the final copy of the manuscript in Desktop Publishing format.

Phyliss Hasse deserves special recognition for providing secretarial support: typing of the original instrument, manuscript, and revisions, preparing the final draft of the manuscript, and maintaining patience and good humor throughout a lengthy and sometimes frustrating process.

PART I:

**OVERVIEW AND PROFILES
OF ACADEMIC LEADERS, THEIR
INSTRUCTIONAL UNITS, AND
THEIR CAMPUSES**

CHAPTER ONE

Overview
of the Study

Education beyond the high school level in the United States has grown in both complexity and comprehensiveness during the past century (Adelman, 1992). Competing for resources with training institutions and traditional four-year colleges and universities, the community college has emerged as one of the premier leaders in educational reform at century's end (Brint & Karabel, 1989). The community college has proven to be a dynamic and multi-faceted community-based institution which has displayed a high degree of flexibility in responding to societal needs.

Response to change has, perhaps more than any other single factor, differentiated two-year, postsecondary from traditional four-year higher education. These postsecondary institutions have experienced unprecedented growth and support from both community groups and business and industry, particularly with respect to their important role in providing mid-career job training. An ability to change rapidly and in direct response to client demand has set the community college in a unique leadership position within the current tide of postsecondary educational reform (Goldenberg, 1990). This educational revolution, in which community colleges played such a vital role, is nearly over, and community colleges now provide classes at nearly all times and in multiple locations throughout the community (Cohen & Brawer, 1989).

Given this dynamic background, the current investigation was undertaken to develop a broader and deeper understanding of academic leadership in community colleges. The foci of this study were to describe results obtained from the CSHPE study, and suggest some of the more obvious implications which arose from the data. Others can certainly be drawn by the reader which make sense to a specific or particular situation or context. The intent was not to thoroughly analyze or interpret the issues, but rather to present data in a concise and understandable manner. Specifically, the purposes for conducting this investigation were three-fold:

- To develop a profile of the characteristics of the chair position, instructional unit, and institution;
- To identify some implications for leadership development of chairs and potential chairs, as well as policy and structural considerations for community colleges.
- To identify areas for more in-depth future research.

Dynamic State of Community Colleges

Educational systems go through stages in a development process, and the community college system has passed through the emerging and developmental stages and is now in the refinement period. Board members, administrators, faculty, and support staff no longer look at growth as the major priority but rather search for methods of providing better services and more effective use of limited financial resources.

The community college has assumed a leadership role in the reconceptualization of how higher education is offered in the United States. Higher education must respond to new technology, abilities, and expectations, and must coordinate these roles with evolving mission and purpose statements (Foster, 1992; Parnell, 1990). While community colleges have entered into articulation agreements for vocational programs, largely through the tech-prep provisions in the 1990 Perkins legislation, community colleges have increased their efforts in providing continuing, business, and transfer education programming (Miller, Edmunds, & Mahler, 1992). As demands for public accountability are at an all-time high, this re-framing of the role and mission of the community college is at the forefront of administrative concerns.

Community colleges have not wholly abandoned vocational or applied education programs, but now have entered into the debate over the mission or expectations of the community college, and who is to pay for these services. Cohen and Brawer ask, "should community colleges educate for further studies, or should they be the capstone for graded education?" (1989, p. 24). It has been suggested that some of the challenges facing the community colleges are: resolving the mission dilemma; evaluating the quality and outcomes of programs; planning for the future; balancing flexibility and responsiveness to social change with institutional integrity; and continuing commitment to the communities community colleges serve (Cross & Fideler, 1989; Deegan, Tillery, & Melone, 1985). These challenges enjoin community college leaders to re-examine programs, priorities, and costs.

While administrators at all levels in a community college must respond to these issues, it is at the department or division level that the responses which affect the lives of students and staff are most directly shaped. Seven to 75 (with an estimated average of 21) divisions and departments exist per community college in the United States (Tucker, 1992). The chair/head of this instructional unit must often negotiate the terms of the response to societal needs, and has a vital role to play in establishing the direction, facilitating the operation, and determining the future of the unit. The department chair may also have responsibility for contact with external and consumer groups and is often seen as the "point-person" in identifying areas in need of change.

Unfortunately, these instructional units operate with the guidance and direction of heads or chairs who, until recently, have been unnoticed in both scholarly and professional literature (Seagren & Miller, 1994). Despite the lack of attention given individual chairs, the importance and vitality of chairing an instructional unit in a community college has been addressed (Tucker, 1992), and the position has been identified as a topic for increased applied research (Carroll & Gmelch, 1992).

Importance of the Chair Position

The department chair plays a vital role in the functions and success of higher education institutions (Seagren, Creswell, & Wheeler, 1993). Chairs have regular contact with administrators, faculty and students. They oversee the department or division's daily operations. They negotiate among unit goals, individual staff goals, and institutional goals. They participate in key decisions, and have authority and responsibility for decisions about students, curriculum, budget, and staffing. While the roles, tasks, and responsibilities of the chair are numerous and well documented, chair practice remains ambiguous and fraught with conflicting interests (Gmelch & Burns, 1991). Although community college chairs may see their role as primarily that of an "administrator," (Tucker, 1992), they are charged with both representing administrative and faculty views and actions. This ambiguity provides both tremendous challenge, opportunity, and role strain (Simpson, 1984).

The challenges facing the chair position relate primarily to the use of interpersonal communication skills for conflict resolution and the professional development of faculty (Murray, 1992). Chairs must resolve conflict and differences of opinion between administration and faculty, students and faculty, and among faculty. Additionally, chairs must find ways of channeling faculty expertise into appropriate developmental tracks or programs to enhance both technical knowledge and teaching ability.

The opportunities related to the chair position are numerous. Chairs hold the key position in relation to promoting excellence in teaching, scholarship, and service, and are situated to manage administrative effectiveness and efficiency. Recognizing the political nature of the campus and surrounding community, chairs are also placed in the unique position of being able to respond to consumer demands while maintaining academic integrity (Kaikai & Kaikai, 1990).

In essence, the chair position has primary responsibility for the academic quality, culture, and operation of the department. This position, then, is crucial to institutional and unit planning, policy and outcomes.

Importance of Leadership Development

Academic institutions have been classified as loosely coupled, political, and bureaucratic institutions (Birnbaum, 1988). The additional pressures of cost constraints, public accountability, increased regulation, and faculty shortages in some areas have added to the complexity of higher education. Within this framework, there has been a growing need to re-cast the academic leader as a business operations officer first, who also understands and encourages faculty development and growth. The need for excellence in dealing with this complexity has been channeled into the growing field of academic leadership development.

Leadership development was once almost exclusively thought of in terms of behavioralist theory, but has evolved to encompass a number of different theories, and has embraced the entire rubric of personal and professional development. Leadership development entails attention to communications abilities and the skills necessary to perform as an administrator of non-human resources. One national study of the in-service needs of community college chairpersons, completed during the period of substantial growth, showed a need for development in chairs' general knowledge of the community college; managerial, personnel and administrative skills; curriculum and instruction issues; and student personnel services (Hammons & Wallace, 1977). A similar study completed among Nebraska community college leaders reinforced the importance of the practice of human relations and personnel administration tasks, and the desire for training related to curriculum and instruction tasks (French, 1980). Because these studies were conducted several years ago, and significant changes have taken place, a need existed to conceptualize a study of the situation in the early part of the decade of the 90s.

Effective leadership development challenges and supports the growth of individuals to prepare them for professional positions of importance and responsibility. Such positions prove to be especially vital in leading faculty and staff at the department or division level, building consensus for effective planning and decision making and designing quality programs which respond to student and community needs.

Conceptual Framework of the Study

The importance of the dynamic environment of community colleges, the central role of departments and divisions in responding to the challenges of this environment, the pivotal position of chairpersons and their continuing need for leadership development contributed to the need for this study.

A conceptual framework was designed to address the multi-faceted environment in which chairpersons work and exercise leadership; it is presented in **Figure 1.1**. Utilizing existing studies and empirical feedback through interviews and discussion groups with community college practitioners and scholars, a four-dimensional model was developed. The four primary components included were the personal characteristics of the chair, responsibilities of the position, challenges of the position, and response strategies used by chairs. In addition to the four primary components, sub-topics or related factors affecting the chair's development and leadership were identified. The resulting conceptual framework allowed for a better understanding of chairs, and their units, institutions, and professional development needs.

Figure 1.1

Conceptual Model of Department Chair Career

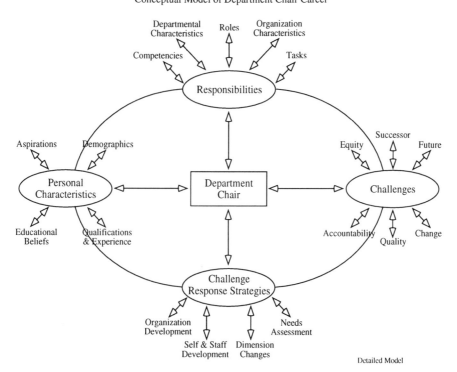

National Study

Although academic community college administrators have been studied in past national surveys (Moore, Twombly, & Martorana, 1985) and department chairs in four-year institutions have been extensively investigated (Seagren, Creswell, & Wheeler, 1993), few efforts have focused solely on the community college department chair (Seagren & Miller, 1994). Recognizing the importance of the chair as an instructional leader and administrator, additional data and exploration were needed about this position in community colleges. Coupling this need for an expanded data base with institutional networking, the Maricopa Community College in Phoenix, Arizona, initiated the National Community College Chair Academy (NCCCA). The Academy has as its primary purpose the professional development of chairs, and seeks the development or enhancement of a knowledge and practitioner base to more effectively address these chair needs. To that end, the Academy contracted with the Center for the Study of Higher and Postsecondary Education (CSHPE) at the University of Nebraska-Lincoln (UN-L) to develop a survey of community college chairs in the U.S. and Canada.

The investigation designed was based upon survey research methods and was intended to be exploratory in nature. It was felt that baseline information was needed about the chairs to establish a profile of characteristics of chairs as well as to determine the need for leadership skills and professional development. The breadth of community college services and programs, combined with the exploratory nature of the study, required the review of a number of survey and research instruments used in previous studies.

Through the identification of chair expectations and role pressures, two primary themes were identified: the need for chair leadership development and the need for appropriate policy and structures within the community college. The study was developed to reflect these themes.

Survey Content

In order to include the components identified in the conceptual model of the chair position, a nine section survey was developed (see Appendix A). The first section of the survey was structured to identify the "characteristics of instructional units." This section of the survey was based on items developed by CSHPE at UN-L, characteristics mentioned in Adelman's 1992 study, and typical demographic information collected by the National Center for Educational Statistics of the U.S. Department of Education.

The second section of the survey included the "characteristics of the respondents' campuses." The items included in the section were developed by the staff of the CSHPE. Additionally, the staff of the NCCCA provided input and modification of the items to accurately reflect the current reality of community colleges.

The third section of the survey collected "personal, demographic" information on the respondents. These typical demographic items have been used in similar national and international studies and were developed by the CSHPE staff based on items used in an earlier department chair study (Creswell, Wheeler, Seagren, Egly, & Beyer, 1990).

The fourth section of the survey dealt with the "educational beliefs and values" of instructional unit heads. These survey items were originally adapted from institutional performance questions included in the 1989 Carnegie Foundation for the Advancement of Teaching survey of faculty. Items were also included from CSHPE research projects with local community colleges, and NCCCA practitioner-based experiences.

The fifth section of the survey collected data on the chairperson "role." The roles identified in the survey were a combination of those advanced by Tucker (1984) and CSHPE's earlier Lilly/TIAA-CREF research project (see Creswell et al., 1990).

The sixth section of the survey dealt with the perceived "tasks" of a department chair. The comprehensive listing included a compilation of those identified by varied authors: tasks and duties (Tucker, 1984), chair skills (Jennerich, 1981), administrative duties of chairs (Smart & Elton, 1976), duties, satisfactions, and goals for the academic role of the chair (McLaughlin, Montgomery, & Malpass, 1975), tasks and responsibilities for the chair in colleges of education (Norton, 1980), and management practices in higher education (Seagren, 1978).

The seventh section of the survey addressed the "skills" necessary for chairing an instructional unit. These questions were based on the skills and competencies utilized by the National Association of Secondary School Principals' Assessment Center Project, directed by the National Association of Secondary School Principals (NASSP, 1992).

The final two sections of the survey, which dealt with "job challenges" and "strategies" to address these challenges, were developed by CSHPE staff. In particular, these questions were identified through applied research with local community colleges with additional input from the NCCCA.

Survey Methods

Upon completion of a draft of the survey, feedback was sought as to the accuracy and comprehensiveness of the instrument. After making minor revisions for clarification, the survey was pilot-tested with selected leaders in Nebraska Community Colleges, student practitioners enrolled in the Educational Leadership and Higher Education doctoral program at UN-L, and participants in the 1992 Institute for Academic Leadership Development sponsored by the NCCCA. Results from the pilot-test provided input for revision, clarification and comprehensiveness.

A listing of potential survey respondents was compiled by the NCCCA by consulting community college catalogs. The listing included the heads or chairs of all instructional units and academic departments in all community colleges in the United States and Canada. The total population was 9,000. Given the exploratory purpose for conducting the investigation, the entire population was selected for study. The instrument was duplicated and mailed to the 9,000 chairs by the NCCCA in September 1992.

In October and November 1992, three follow-up mailings were completed to maximize the number of respondents. A total of 3,000 survey response sheets were received, including 2,875 usable returns, yielding a response rate of 32%. Wave analysis, a common statistical procedure used to test for response bias by late participants, indicated that these responses were indicative of the types of responses that would have been received from the entire population. The data were compiled from the response sheets by NCCCA support services at the Maricopa Community Colleges and sent to the CSHPE staff for statistical analysis and the development of the final report. A more detailed discussion about the data analysis is presented in Appendix B.

Summary

The community college has assumed a leading role among institutions of postsecondary education in responding to change. As community colleges face change, the department (or division) chair position has taken on an increasingly important role. The chair has daily contact with faculty, students, and administrators, and is subsequently seen as the individual most responsible for assuring academic quality.

An analysis of existing literature and research provided the basis for the development of the conceptual model of the chair position used in this study. The model included four components: the characteristics of the chair, responsibilities of the position, challenges of the position, and response strategies used by chairs.

The investigation was conducted with three guiding purposes:
- develop a profile of the characteristics of the chair position, instructional unit, and institution;

- identify implications for leadership development and for the policy and structure of community colleges; and,
- identify areas for future study and understanding.

These three purposes also provide the framework for the remaining chapters of the book.

CHAPTER TWO

Characteristics of the Chair

What is the profile of the approximately 3,000 chairs who responded to the survey? An important dimension of understanding any population is identifying characteristics of its members through research. No national profile exists of chairs in the community colleges, although profiles exist for community college chairs in a few states. For example, one study in Mississippi showed that the typical chairperson in a public junior college was male, white, and middle-aged (Broadway, 1984). In another example, from Illinois, male chairs outnumbered female chairs by four times, and the modal age was between 40-49 years (Simpson, 1984). A 1979 Nebraska study which explored these personal characteristics also found 80% of the chairs were male and 20% female, however the model age was between 35 and 44 years (French, 1980).

This chapter reviews the profile of demographic and position characteristics of the chairs from the national survey, in three sections: personal characteristics, experience, and type of appointment. Data about these characteristics are important in order to develop a profile of the community college chair, and to provide insights and understandings which can be useful in designing and developing training materials and programs for academic leadership development. With the changing nature of community colleges, the need for creative and dynamic leadership is critical, and the profile of the present chairs can provide a basis for the recruitment of chairs for the future.

What Chairs Said

Personal Characteristics

Personal characteristic items included on the survey were age, gender, race, and educational preparation. As shown in **Table 2.1**, less than 1% of the individuals occupying the position of chair were under 30 years of age, and slightly more than 2% were over 65 years of age. The average age fell within the category 45-54 years; 46.9% of the respondents were in this category, 27.0% in the category 30-44 and 23.5% in the category 56-64 years of age. Thus, the distribution of the chairs' age responses was a bell-shaped curve. Nearly three-quarters of the chairs were 45 years of age or older. If the average high school graduate is 18 years old, the majority of chairs had 27 to 47 years in some type of position after high school graduation. A comparative analysis showed that female chairs were slightly younger than their male counterparts: 34.4% were younger than 45, 44.8% in the 45 to 54 age category and only 21.8% over 55. The breakdown for male chairs was 22.4% under 45, 48.9% in the 45 to 54 category and 28.6% over 55 years of age.

Table 2.1: Personal Characteristics of Respondents in Study

Characteristics	Categories	Percentage Response	Mean
Your age	Under 30	.4	45-54
	30-44	27.0	
	45-54	46.9	
	55-64	23.5	
	65 & Over	2.1	
Your gender	Female	40.7	
	Male	59.3	
Your race	Native American, Canadian Aleut, Eskimo Inuit	3.5	
	Asian or Pacific Islander (Japanese, Chinese, Filipino, Asian Indian, Korean, Vietnamese, Hawaiian, Guamanian, Samoan, other Asian)	1.4	
	Black/African American	3.6	
	White	89.3	
	Hispanic/Latino	1.8	
	Other	.4	
Highest academic degree you have achieved	Less than baccalaureate	3.3	
	Baccalaureate	9.2	
	Masters	59.3	
	Specialist Certificate/Degree	4.6	
	Doctorate	23.6	

Figure 2.1 clearly portrays that nearly one-quarter of the existing chairs will need to be replaced in the next 10 years, and nearly three-quarters in the next 20 years, if the average age of retirement remains 65.

Figure 2.1

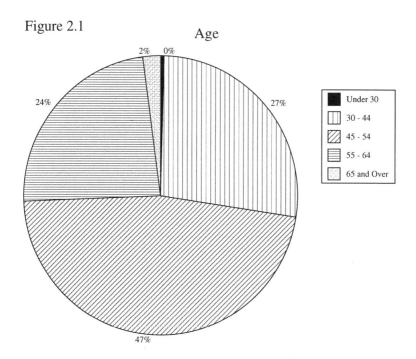

In terms of gender, 40.7% of respondents were female and 59.3% were male. These data indicate a real effort has been made to provide equal opportunity for both men and women in leadership positions in community colleges. When compared to data for chairs in four-year institutions, these data are especially impressive, as only 14% of the chairs in one study of four-year institutions were female while 86% were male (Vavrus, Grady, & Creswell, 1988). Compared to other higher education, the community colleges should be given high marks for providing equal opportunity for females and males in leadership positions.

In terms of race, 89.3% of the chairs were Caucasian and 10.7% were members of one of the ethnic minority groups identified on the survey. Two groups were equally represented, Native American, Canadian Aleut, or Eskimo Inuit (3.5%) and Black/African American (3.5%). Other groups identified included Hispanic and Latino chairs (1.8%), and Asian or Pacific Islander chairs (1.4%). These data indicate a real opportunity and need for future leadership development for members of ethnic minority groups. The need for cultural role models in leadership positions, and the career paths to such positions is only beginning to be studied in community colleges (Johnson, 1991). Considerable effort will need to be expended to gain an understanding and provide educational and leadership opportunities for ethnic involvement. Recruitment of members of ethnic minority groups is especially important for community colleges to provide opportunities for upward mobility, improve job opportunities and provide opportunities for those interested in transferring to four-year institutions.

The individuals holding chair positions in community colleges were highly educated, with 9.2% holding a baccalaureate degree, 59.3% a masters degree, 4.6% a specialist certificate, and 23.6% a doctorate.

Experience

Survey items related to previous experience included on the survey were community college faculty member, chair, or other administrator, and positions outside of the community college in business, other educational institutions, or public/governmental agencies. Experience is a great teacher (Dewey, 1963), especially for individuals who occupy leadership positions or assume leadership roles (Creswell et al., 1990). Thus, chairs need to learn from experience in order to have an understanding of problems faced, opportunities available, and challenges in the position. **Figure 2.2** shows the range of experiences of the chairs. **Table 2.2** shows responses by the number and average number of years in specific positions.

Virtually all of the chairs (96.9%) had been faculty members prior to assuming the position of chair. The average number of years of experience as a faculty member fell within the 11-15 year category, and over 80% of the chairs had six or more years of such experience. Because the individuals who occupy the chair position have considerable experience as faculty members, they are in a strong position to understand and appreciate faculty needs, motivations, and expectations.

With respect to experience as a chair, only 1.3% were in their first year, so nearly 99% had one or more years of experience as a chair. The highest percentage of chairs indicated 1-5 years of experience (44.8%), but the average fell within the 6-10 year category. The average number of years of other types of administrative experiences within community colleges was 1-5 years, however, only one-third of the chairs had such experience.

Figure 2.2

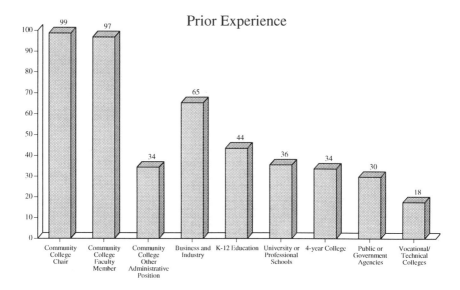

Table 2.2: Experience Characteristics of Respondents in Study

Characteristics	Categories	Percentage Response	Mean
Number of years of **your** professional experience working in community colleges as a faculty member	No experience	3.1	11-15 years
	1-5 years	12.0	
	6-10 years	16.8	
	11-15 years	19.8	
	16-20 years	19.5	
	Over 20 years	28.8	

Table 2.2: Experience Characteristics of Respondents in Study (cont'd)

Characteristics	Categories	Percentage Response	Mean
Number of years of **your** professional experience working in community colleges as **a chair or head** (or comparable position)	No experience	1.3	6-10 years
	1-5 years	44.8	
	6-10 years	26.2	
	11-15 years	14.8	
	16-20 years	7.1	
	Over 20 years	5.8	
Number of years of **your** professional experience working in community colleges in **other administrative positions**	No experience	65.6	1-5 years
	1-5 years	24.9	
	6-10 years	4.8	
	11-15 years	1.9	
	16-20 years	1.2	
	Over 20 years	1.6	
Do you have prior experience working in business/industry?	Yes	65.4	
	No	34.6	
Do you have prior experience working in K-12 schools?	Yes	43.5	
	No	56.5	
Do you have prior experience working in other public agencies (e.g., government agencies)?	Yes	29.7	
	No	70.3	

Table 2.2: Experience Characteristics of Respondents in Study (cont'd)

Characteristics	Categories	Percentage Response	Mean
Do you have prior experience working in a university of professional school?	Yes	35.5	
	No	64.5	
Do you have prior experience working in a vocational/technical college or institute?	Yes	17.5	
	No	82.5	

Regarding prior work experience in business and industry, 65.4% of the chairs indicated that they had worked in such settings. However, 83.4% of the chairs of business administration and accounting programs and 76.0% of the chairs of nursing and allied health programs had prior business experience.

In terms of experience prior to becoming a community college chair in other types of educational institutions, 43.5% of the chairs had been in K-12 schools, 33.6% in four-year colleges, 35.5% in a university or professional school, and 17.5% in vocational and technical schools. In addition, 29.7% had prior experience in public or nonprofit agencies, including governmental agencies. Thus, as a group the chairs had extensive experience either as a faculty member, in business and industry, or in some other type of educational or non-profit setting. These data provide strong indications that chairs in community colleges assume their leadership responsibility with a solid experience base from which to provide leadership for the faculty, to understand organizations and to build relationships with business and industry.

Appointment

Appointment items included in the survey were stipend received, type of appointment, length of term of appointment, the amount of release time received, the annual salary, and professional plans for the future. **Table 2.3** lists responses to the survey and the averages for questions related to the chairperson's appointment.

Table 2.3: Appointment Characteristics of Respondents in Study

Characteristics	Categories	Percentage Response	Mean
Is your appointment as chair or head (or comparable position) limited to a specific term?	Yes	35.1	
	No	64.9	
If yes, length of the term	Less than 3 years	50.6	
	3 years	43.0	
	More than 3 years	6.4	
If yes, is the appointment renewable?	Yes	96.9	
	No	3.1	
Do you receive reassigned or released time from teaching for being a chair?	Yes	73.2	
	No	26.8	
If yes, how much time is reassigned or released in terms of a 3-credit hour semester or quarter courses?	1 class	27.3	3 classes
	2 classes	26.9	
	3 classes	15.6	
	4 classes	10.1	
	5 classes	3.1	
	Full time	17.0	

Table 2.3: Appointment Characteristics of Respondents in Study (cont'd)

Characteristics	Categories	Percentage Response	Mean
Do you receive a stipend for being a chair or head (or comparable position)	Yes	58.0	
	No	42.0	
If yes, how much (on an annual basis)?	$500 or less	8.0	$1501-2000
	$501-1000	13.9	
	$1001-1500	17.5	
	$1501-2000	11.7	
	$2001-2500	11.7	
	Over $2500	37.3	
Your annual salary	$20000 or less	.6	$41000-60000
	$21000-40000	29.5	
	$41000-60000	55.6	
	$6100-80000	13.7	
	Over $80000	.6	
Average number of hours you work in a typical week as a chair or head (or comparable position)	10 or less	9.4	31-40 hours per week
	11-20	19.4	
	21-30	12.7	
	31-40	19.3	
	41-50	29.6	
	51-60	9.5	

Table 2.3: Appointment Characteristics of Respondents in Study (cont'd)

Characteristics	Categories	Percentage Response	Mean
Your professional plans in the next five years	Stay at same community college	73.9	
	Move to another community college	4.9	
	Move to a 4-year institution of higher education	2.9	
	Move to a position in non-profit, private sector	1.3	
	Retire	13.3	
	Other	3.7	
If you plan to stay in **community colleges**, what are your career plans for the next five years?	Not applicable	14.2	
	Remain in chair position	54.4	
	Move to a faculty position	11.3	
	Move to another administrative position	17.3	
	Other	2.8	
If you plan to move to another administrative position at a community college, what is the position to which you aspire?	Not applicable	75.7	
	Dean	14.5	
	Vice-president	3.8	
	Campus president	1.4	
	System chancellor	.2	
	Other	4.3	

Nearly two-thirds of the chairs indicated their appointment was not limited to a specific term (64.9%). For the one-third who indicated their appointment was limited to a specific term, 50.6% indicated it was limited to less than three years, 43.0% to three years, and 6.4% to more than 3 years. However, 96.9% of his group indicated their appointment could be renewed. Therefore, less than 2.0% of all survey respondents were precluded from remaining in their chair role for as long as they remained effective and elected to retain the position. These data present a different picture from that found in a national study of chairs in four-year institutions in which two-thirds of the chairs had appointments of specific terms, the appointments ranged from one to six years in duration, and the position was not seen as a career position (Vavrus, Grady, & Creswell, 1988; Creswell et al., 1990). The data related to appointment would seem to indicate that the community college chair position was far more often seen as a career position; even in cases where the appointment was limited to a specific term, it could be renewed. Such career potential points to the chair position as providing opportunity for leadership continuity within the community college. This situation conversely suggests some constraints on the ability of the community college to encourage and recruit individuals to assume leadership positions, and may actually discourage some who would otherwise aspire to assume these positions in the future. However, given the age of the present chairs and the number of replacements which will be required, it appears there will be adequate opportunity and real need for community colleges to begin to identify, recruit, and prepare individuals to assume the chair position. Recruitment of potential chairs from the faculty can have positive implications, but can negatively impact both the number and quality of remaining faculty members.

Figure 2.3 shows that the amount of release time chairs were given to devote to the responsibility of being a chair varied. Nearly three-fourths of the chairs (73.2%) were given some release time from teaching responsibilities to devote to chair responsibilities. The normal teaching load for full-time community college faculty is five classes per semester. The amount of release time received ranged from one class to five classes, with an average of three classes. Over one-half of the chairs had release time of one or two classes, over one-quarter had three to five classes, and 17% had full release time. The size of the unit had a significant impact on the amount of release time. Understandably chairs in larger units had the greatest amount of release time. In instructional units with a student headcount of fewer than 400, the average release time fell between two to three classes, but the majority of the chairs had one or two classes. For units of over 800 students, the average fell between three to four classes, but the majority of chairs had release time of two to three classes.

Figure 2.3

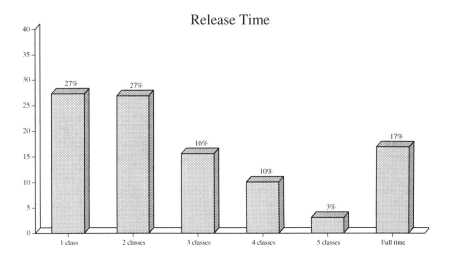

Is there a monetary reward for assuming the leadership responsibilities of chair? A majority of respondents (58.0%) received a stipend for the chair's responsibility. The stipend amount varied considerably, ranging from $500 or less to over $2,500 per year, as shown in **Figure 2.4**. Over $2,500 was received by 37.3% of the respondents, however, the average stipend fell in the $1,500-2,000 category. Again, an increased unit size corresponded to a higher stipend received. The average stipend for chairs of instructional units of less than 400 students fell between the $1,001-1,500 and $1,501-2,000 categories. Conversely, the average stipend for chairs in units of 800 or more students fell between the two categories $1,501-2,000 and $2,001-2,500. The most frequent response of these chairs was over $2,400 (51.2%).

The next area of the survey related to total compensation received for being a chair, along with any other roles. The range in salary for the chair was from $20,000 or less to over $80,000, as shown in **Figure 2.5**, however only a small percentage of chairs were at these levels. Less than one percent received $20,000 or less (.6%), and less than one percent received over $80,000 (.6%). The majority (55.6%) received compensation in the $41,000-60,000 range; 29.5% received $21,000-40,000; and 13.7% received $61,000-80,000. The average salary fell in the $41,000-60,000 range.

Figure 2.4

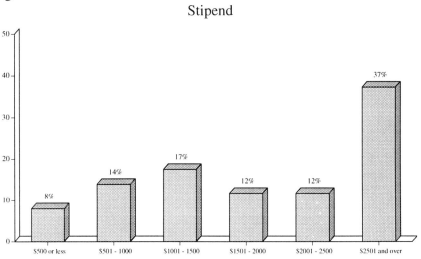

Stipend

Figure 2.5

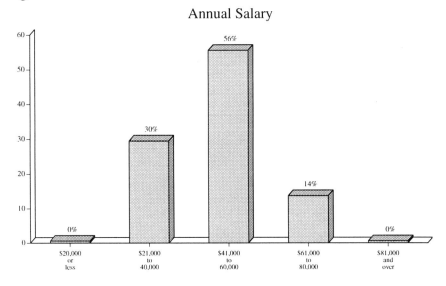

Annual Salary

The number of hours per week spent in chair responsibilities ranged from 10 or less (9.4%) to 51-60 hours (9.5%) as shown in **Figure 2.6**. The average amount of time spent on chair responsibilities was 31-40 hours per week, but nearly one-third of the chairs indicated 41-50 hours per week were spent on these responsibilities (29.6%). The size of the instructional unit also impacted the number of hours spent on chair responsibilities. The average for chairs in units of less than 400 students was between the 21-30 and the 31-40 hour categories, while the average for chairs of units of more than 800 students fell in the 31-40 hour category. For chairs in units of fewer than 400 students, 32.7% reported 41 or more hours of work, while 46.6% of the chairs in units of over 800 students reported working 41 or more hours each week. Given the previously stated fact that only 17% of the chairs were released full time for chair responsibilities, it is clear chair responsibilities demand a time commitment well beyond the normal 40-hour week. These results support other studies of chairpersons. In one report on chairpersons, the "administrative professor" worked an average of 56.4 hours per week, thus putting in more overtime than any other occupational group, even physicians (Gmelch & Miskin, 1993).

Figure 2.6

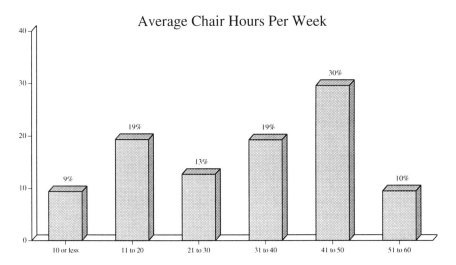

The future professional plans of individuals occupying the position of chair indicate considerable stability. The data in **Figure 2.7** show 74% planned to stay in the same community college for the next five years. Of that group, 54% indicated they planned to remain as a chair for the next five years, 11% planned to return to the faculty and 17% planned to move to another administrative position. Of those who planned to move to another administrative position, 15% indicated they planned to move to the dean's position. Only 4% were interested in becoming a vice president, 1.4% a campus president, and .2% a system chancellor.

Figure 2.7

Plans for the Future

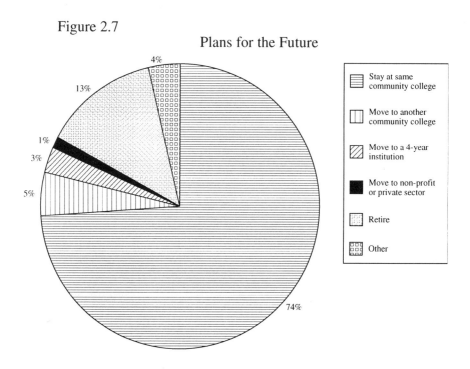

Legend:
- Stay at same community college
- Move to another community college
- Move to a 4-year institution
- Move to non-profit or private sector
- Retire
- Other

Pie chart values: 4%, 13%, 1%, 3%, 5%, 74%

Summary

The purpose of this chapter was to develop a profile of the chairs of community colleges. The demographics of the chairs indicate that these individuals are middle age or older, there is an almost equal number of males and females in the chair positions, and the chairs are predominately white and highly educated with 88% having a degree beyond the baccalaureate. The group had a wide range of experiences prior to assuming the role of chair. Nearly all had been a faculty member in a community college, nearly two-thirds had worked in business and industry, and one-third or more had experiences in other educational institutions such as K-12 or four year colleges and universities. The chairs either had appointments with unlimited terms, or if a term was specified it could be renewed. Most of the chairs were given some release time from teaching responsibilities to devote to chair responsibilities. The chairs received an extra stipend for being chair which ranged from $500 or less to over $2500 with an average of $1500-2000. Their average salaries fell in the $40,000-60,000 range. The chairs worked an average of 31-40 hours per week specifically on chair responsibilities. The size of the unit had an impact with chairs in larger units receiving more release time, larger stipends, larger salaries, and spending a greater number of hours per week on chair responsibilities. Most chairs plan to stay in the community colleges, as well as in the chair position, for the immediate (5 year) future.

Implications for Leadership Development

• Because of the age of the individuals currently occupying chair positions, there is a need for academic leadership development training for a large number of faculty who will be needed to replace retiring chairs over the next two decades.

• There is an equally pressing need for continued training for the third of chairs who are under 45 years of age, and may serve more than 20 additional years as chair. Because of the commitment of these chairs and their plans to stay at the same institution and in the same role, community colleges should invest and provide resources for leadership development for this group.

• Because of the small number of chairs representing ethnic minority and cultural groups, considerable effort and resources need to be expended to identify, select, and train such individuals to prepare them for leadership positions in community colleges. Ethnic chairs can be positive role models which will assist in recruitment and retention of ethnic minority students and faculty. Community colleges should continue to make a concerted effort to provide leadership opportunities equally for males, females, and people from the various cultural groups.

• Since many of those in chair positions, particularly in the health, business, and technical areas, have come to their positions without a background in education or educational administration, leadership development programs should be comprehensive including education philosophy, theory, process, and administration.

• The community college faculty should be the major source for identifying and recruiting individuals with leadership potential to participate in academic leadership development programs. Additionally, leadership skills can be developed for these individuals through participation in committee and task force assignments, selected administrative duties, and other internal leadership training opportunities.

• Business and industry is another source for identifying individuals with leadership potential, and an interest in education, who might be willing to consider a career change. Leaders from business and industry can be identified and recruited through their involvement in advisory committees, governing boards, program reviews, and other activities which bring them in contact with the community college. These individuals, too, could participate in a range of different types of academic leadership development programs.

• Academic leadership development programs need to utilize the advantages and strengths of a wide range of programs. These might include professional association, offerings, formal graduate courses and professional development programs offered by selected disciplines. In addition, existing programs specifically focused on leadership development for academic leaders in community colleges should be explored.

Implications for Policy and Campus Structure

• Community colleges need to consider the adequacy of the release time given to chairs, because reported release time does not approximate the time chairs report spending on chairing responsibilities. Procedures for systematically assessing workload need to be developed, as there are a number of factors which can contribute to an individual chair needing more or less release time.

• Community colleges should review salary guidelines or structures to determine that both compensation and extra stipends are consistent with levels of responsibility and the time commitments of the chair position.

• Community colleges need to explore, design, and deliver "in house" professional development programs which meet the unique and specific needs of faculty and administration.

• Community colleges should examine the politics concerning the type of appointment provided to chairs: continuous versus rotational. The type of leadership development needs and the type of responsibilities assigned are influenced by the system of appointment employed.

• Community colleges need to review the age, experience, and future plans of the current chairs, to determine the need for policies which may encourage early retirement incentives to assure some degree of continuity in the combined leadership of chairs of an entire campus.

• Community colleges should emphasize the importance of providing equal leadership opportunities for both men and women. Community colleges should identify and provide leadership training opportunities to increase the number of ethnic minority chairs.

CHAPTER THREE

Characteristics of Instructional Units and Their Campuses

What is the profile of the instructional unit and campus where chairs work? Community and junior colleges exist within the extremely broad framework of "postsecondary" education. Because they do not fall under the type of state control typical of K-12 schools, community colleges have a great deal of autonomy and responsibility to design programs to meet the needs of their local communities, businesses and industries, and students. This lack of centralized decision-making, strong local focus, and wide range of clientele served make it difficult to describe a "typical" campus or its individual academic units. This chapter examines 21 characteristics or aspects of the instructional units and campuses, and demonstrates the wide range of unit and campus types.

Community colleges evolved from the tradition of normal teacher training schools, and their academic units or departments originated in the pattern of others in higher education (Garms, 1977). The creation of these special purpose colleges and departments enabled faculty to further specialize, but this development created a need for capable administrators to oversee academic and business operations of these units. Through a century of existence, departments have evolved into politically charged clusters of programs, resources, faculty, and students. Both campuses and departments have been described as thriving on organized anarchy and political positioning (Birnbaum, 1988). Surprisingly, little is known about the instructional units in community colleges. Tucker's (1992) research provided some information; for example he estimated an average of 21 departments/divisions per campus.

The CSHPE survey included items related to both the instructional unit and the community college campus. Using categorical responses, nine items were provided to define the characteristics of instructional units, and 12 items were used to collect information on campus characteristics.

What Chairs Said

Instructional Units

As shown in **Table 3.1**, survey results indicated the average department chair was responsible for 401-600 students and 11-20 full-time faculty in a unit that had existed for 16-20 years. The majority of respondents (64.5%) held the title of chair, while 12.3% responded that they were called a coordinator/director. A smaller percentage of respondents indicated that they held the position of both chair and head (9.2%), head (7.7%), assistant or associate dean (3.5%), or other (2.9%).

Table 3.1: Characteristics of Instructional Unit

Characteristics	Categories	Percentage Response	Mean
Your present position	Chair	64.5	
	Head	7.7	
	Both head and chair	9.2	
	Coordinator/Director	12.3	
	Asst/Assoc Dean	3.5	
	Other	2.9	
Name of the instructional unit for which you are responsible	Department	56.8	
	Division	35.7	
	Area	2.4	
	Specialization	2.3	
	Other	2.9	
Student headcount (full + part-time in your unit	200 or less	26.5	401-600
	201-400	15.8	
	401-600	10.6	
	601-800	8.2	
	801-1000	6.3	
	Over 1000	32.6	
Full-time faculty (headcount) in your unit	10 or less	56.3	11-20
	11-20	26.7	
	21-30	9.7	
	31-40	3.2	
	41-50	1.7	
	Over 50	2.4	

Table 3.1: Characteristics of Instructional Unit (cont'd)

Characteristics	Categories	Percentage Response	Mean
Part-time faculty (headcount) in your unit	10 or less	49.9	11-20
	11-20	20.8	
	21-30	10.2	
	31-40	7.2	
	41-50	4.3	
	Over 50	7.6	
Years your unit has been operating as an instructional unit	Less than 1 year	1.9	16-20
	1-5 years	12.0	
	6-10 years	11.5	
	11-15 years	11.1	
	16-20 years	16.0	
	More than 20 years	47.4	
Indicate the type of degree most commonly conferred on graduates from your unit: For **United States** units only	Assoc of Arts	37.6	
	Assoc of Sciences	18.9	
	Assoc of Applied Sciences	30.0	
	Assoc of General Sciences	1.5	
	Diploma or certificate	7.5	
	Other	4.6	
For **Canadian** units only	Certificate	30.8	
	Diploma	44.9	
	Transfer program	10.5	
	B.A. degree	3.3	
	Other	10.1	

Table 3.1: Characteristics of Instructional Unit (cont'd)

Characteristics	Categories	Percentage Response	Mean
Below are listed program areas in community colleges identified by the American Association of Community Colleges. Identify the program area with the **largest student enrollment** in your unit	Liberal Arts and Sciences	23.2	
	General Studies	8.7	
	Nursing/Allied Health	15.3	
	Business Adm/ Accounting	11.1	
	Office/Business Support	2.4	
	Engineering & Sci Tech	7.0	
	Education/Human Services	3.5	
	Protective Services	1.1	
	Agriculture & Natural Sci	1.4	
	Fine and Performing Arts	3.2	
	Trades/Precision Production	5.0	
	Sciences	3.6	
	Computer Serv Data Prcess	3.6	
	Personal Services	.3	
	Other	9.0	

The majority of instructional units (56.8%) were identified as a department. Academic instructional units were also termed division (35.7%), area (2.4%), or a special or other non-identified name (5.2%). The size of units in terms of full- and part-time student headcounts ranged from 200 or less (26.5%) to over 1000 (32.6%). The average size was from 401-600 students, with 15.8% in the category 201-400, 10.6% in 401-600, 8.2% in 601-800, and 6.3% in the category 801-1000. The size of full-time faculty ranged from 10 or less (56.3%) to over 50 (2.4%). The average size fell within the 11-20 category. So the institutional units are relatively small in terms of full-time faculty. A similar situation existed for part-time faculty, with a range from 10 or less (49.9%), to over 50 (7.6%). The average headcount of 11-20 part-time faculty was the same, and 20.8% of responses fell within this category. No question was asked regarding the F.T.E. for part-time faculty in the unit. Combining the total number of full- and part-time faculty increases the average unit size to a 22-40 faculty headcount. Managing such a work force presents many opportunities and challenges for the chairs to provide leadership.

Most instructional units had been operating for extended periods of time; 47.4% had existed for 20-plus years and the average fell in the 16-20 year category; less than 2% had been operating for less than 1 year; other responses were 1-5 years (12.0%); 6-10 years (11.5%); 11-15 years (11.1%); and 16-20 years (16.0%).

The respondents in the United States indicated that their unit offered either an associate of arts (37.6%) or applied sciences (30.0%) degree. Other degrees conferred included the associates of science (18.9%), diploma or certificate (7.5%), the associates of general studies (1.5%), or an other, non-specified degree (4.6%). Associate of arts degrees were disproportionately awarded in units with the largest enrollment in Liberal Arts and Sciences or General Studies programs, while the applied science associate degree was more frequently offered in Nursing and Allied Health or Business Administration and Accounting programs.

The types of degrees offered by Canadian institutions differ, so a separate question was included on the survey. The majority of these institutions conferred a certificate (30.8%) or diploma (44.9%), while the bachelor of arts degree was offered by 3.3% of the respondents, and transfer program enrollment was offered by 10.5% of respondents.

Respondents also indicated the program area in their department which had the largest enrollment at the time of study. Of the 15 programs listed, Liberal Arts and Sciences was indicated by 23.2% of the respondents, followed by Nursing and Allied Health (15.3%), Business Administration and Accounting (11.1%), Engineering and Science Technology (7.0%), Trade and Precision Production (5.0%), Computer Science and Data Processing (3.6%), Science (3.6%), Education and Human Services (3.5%), Fine and Performing Arts (3.2%), Office and Business Support (2.4%), Agriculture and Natural Sciences (1.4%), Protective Services (1.1%), and Personal Services (.3%). Other non-identified areas totaled 9.0%.

Campuses

As shown in **Table 3.2**, chairs indicated that their campuses had an average full-time enrollment of 4,001-6,000 students and the same average of 4,001-6,000 part-time students. The majority of responding chairs indicated 2,000 or fewer full-time students (33.6%) and 26.4% indicated 2,001-4,000, making a total of 60% of the campuses with less than 4,000 full-time students. With respect to part-time student numbers, nearly half of the respondents indicated 2,000 or fewer part-time students (41.7%) and 18.4% indicated 2,001-4,000, again making a total of 60% of the campuses with less than 4,000 part-time students. Only 11.3% of the respondents indicated 10,000 or more full-time students, and 13.5% indicated as many part-time students.

Table 3.2: Characteristics of Respondent's Campus

Question	Categories	Percentage Response	Mean
Number of **full-time** students (headcount) on your your campus	2000 or less	33.6	4001-6000
	2001-4000	26.4	
	4001-6000	14.5	
	6001-8000	9.2	
	8001-10,000	5.0	
	Over 10,000	11.3	
Number of **part-time** students (headcount) on your campus	2000 or less	41.7	4001-6000
	2001-4000	18.4	
	4001-6000	12.7	
	6001-8000	8.5	
	8001-10,000	5.1	
	Over 10,000	13.5	
Number of **full-time** faculty (headcount) on your campus	50 or less	17.3	101-150
	51-100	26.5	
	101-150	20.0	
	151-200	13.2	
	201-250	9.5	
	Over 250	13.5	
Number of **part-time** faculty (headcount) on your campus	50 or less	23.5	101-150
	51-100	19.2	
	101-150	14.2	
	151-200	9.2	
	201-250	8.5	
	Over 250	25.5	
The number of your chairpersons (or comparable position) on campus	5 or less	21.4	11-20
	6-10	30.0	
	11-20	24.8	
	21-30	12.3	
	31-40	5.7	
	More than 41	5.8	

Table 3.2: Characteristics of Respondent's Campus (Cont'd)

Question	Categories	Percentage Response	Mean
Answer this question only if your campus is a U.S. institution. Accrediting region where your campus is located	New England	5.1	
	Middle States	16.2	
	Southern	33.4	
	North Central	23.2	
	Northwest	6.9	
	Western	15.2	
The instructional focus of your campus	Occupational/Technical	13.3	
	Academic Transfer	8.7	
	Both Technical and Transfer	76.8	
	Other	1.2	
The primary source of your funding	Public	95.8	
	Private	4.2	
If public, degree of funding support from the State or Province	33% or less	21.0	
	34%-66%	29.8	
	67% or more	49.1	
If public, **degree** of funding support from the County/Region	33% or less	82.0	
	34%-66%	15.4	
	67% or more	2.5	
If public, **degree** of funding support from local/city	33% or less	93.3	
	34%-66%	5.1	
	67% or more	1.6	
The individual or group responsible for appointing/electing department or division chairs (or comparable position) after the search process on your campus	Elected by faculty	17.5	
	Appointed by administration	51.8	
	Combination of faculty/administration	29.5	
	Other	1.1	

The average size of full- and part-time faculty on the campus fell within the 101-150 category. If the categories of 50 or less, 51-100, and 101-150 are combined, 60% of the chairs reported a full-time faculty of fewer than 150 persons. If the same categories are combined for part-time faculty, just under 60% of the chairs indicated part-time faculty of this size.

These faculty are guided in their efforts by an average of 11-20 chairs on the campus. Responses ranged from 5 or fewer chairs (21.4%) to 41 or more (5.8), with the most frequent responses of 6-10 chairs (30.0%).

The location of the institutions in terms of U.S. accrediting regions was as follows: 5.1% were in New England, 16.2% were in the Middle States, 33.4% in the Southern region, 23.2% in the North Central region, 6.9% in the Northwest region, and 15.2% in the Western region.

Nearly all of the respondents (95.8%) received their primary funding from public sources, with more than two-thirds of the public funding coming from a state or province for half (49.1%) of the respondents. This is consistent with Cohen and Brawer's (1989) finding that proportions of state aid increased over the period since 1942 from 28% to nearly half in 1986. Public funding from a county or region accounted for 33% or less of the college's revenue, as reported by 82.0% of the respondents. Similarly, 93.3% of the responding chairs received 33% or less of their funding from local or city sources. The community colleges are primarily publicly funded with the majority of support coming from the state, and the balance from the county or region, then local or city sources.

Consistent with the shifting foci of community colleges discussed earlier, there were few campuses which classified themselves as entirely occupational/technical (13.3%) or academic transfer (8.7%). The majority of respondents indicated the instructional focus of their campus was comprehensive, including both academic transfer and technical programs (76.8%). Combining staff members (academic and technical) in a comprehensive community college has the potential for creating philosophical differences. The role, expectations, and responsibilities of chairs are also influenced by these orientations. Continuing dialogue must take place to assist in clarifying such differences and to create an understanding that the institution can be strengthened through the offering of both types of programs.

The largest number of responding chairs (51.8%) indicated that they were appointed to the chair position by the administration. Chair appointment via faculty election accounted for 17.5% of the chair appointments, and 29.5% were appointed by a combination of faculty and administration.

Summary

The profile of the instructional units and the campuses included in this survey indicates an instructional unit typically called a department or division, headed by a chair who has responsibility for 401-600 students, 11-20 full-time faculty, and 11-20 part-time faculty. Although the position title varies across types of institutions, the most popular title in the U.S. as determined in other national studies is that of chair (Seagren, Creswell, & Wheeler, 1993). The majority of the chairs were appointed by the campus administration rather than being elected by the faculty.

These instructional units offered primarily the Associate of Arts or Applied Science Degree, with the largest student enrollment in Liberal Arts and Sciences followed by Nursing and Allied Heath, then Business Administration and Accounting. The majority of the institutional units had been in operation for 16-20 years. The campuses had average of 11-20 chairs, which supports Tucker's (1992) estimate of 20 chairs on each college and university campus. The majority of campuses had 150 or fewer full-time faculty and a similar number of part-time faculty. Most of the chairs reported 4,000 or fewer full-time students and a similar number of part-time students. These institutions were typically public with the majority of funds coming from state or provincial sources and the remainder from county and local resources. Most institutions were comprehensive with instructional foci of both technical and transfer programs.

Implications for Leadership Development

• The unique nature of each community college campus and instructional unit dictates the need for customized internal and external professional development activities. These developmental activities need to include experiences and simulations which reflect varying faculty and student headcounts, as well as vocational and transfer instructional foci.

• Public funding was predominant among respondents and requires that current and future department chairs have adequate training in fiscal management and budgeting behavior. More than the simple knowledge of fiscal issues, chairs must be cognizant of public accountability issues which rise parallel to drawing on the local or state tax base.

• As Creswell et al. (1990) discussed, the chair must be well trained in the art of academic human resource management. These strategies must empower the chair to communicate to both large and small groups, as well as with groups of peers and students. Additionally, leadership development programs should include topics such as adult work motivation, workload assignments and analysis, conflict management and resolution, procedures and processes for developing a learning community, and strategies to develop trust, to better enable the chair to create a positive work environment for the unit.

• Most of the community colleges reported near equal numbers of full- and part-time faculty, and this combination places unique challenges on the chair role which must be addressed. For example, competence in content areas may differ dramatically if part-time faculty are practitioners. These varying levels of knowledge may make it difficult for the chair to design or assess curriculum. The evaluation of part-time faculty may also differ from those strategies used with full-time faculty (Gappa & Leslie, 1993).

• As the chair is often neither full-time administrator or full-time faculty member, it can be a lonely position. Leadership development programs should encourage the development of campus networks of chairs which can not only be a support system for chairs, but can also guide the direction and activities of continuing professional education or leadership development programs. Green and McDade (1991) offer a number of suggestions for such networking.

• The community colleges were located in all crediting regions of the U.S. This distribution suggests that regional issues, such as demographics, or types of business and industry, may best be addressed through regional leadership development programs. Regional programs reduce costs and travel time, allow for specific regional needs to be addressed or considered, and facilitate the sharing of resources on the development of linkages.

Implications for Policy and Campus Structure

• Student enrollment and faculty headcount should be monitored at the departmental level to assure a desired balance between teachers and learners. The department chair must make timely decisions about the faculty-student ratio, and appoint adjunct and part-time instructors to assure the possibility of interaction, if not quality, in the classroom.

• Considering the diverse nature of instructional units, chairs should make efforts to collaborate across disciplines in planning and faculty development. Inter-departmental collaboration can lead to increased understanding of the entire college and a stronger appreciation of the challenges facing administrators.

• With predominantly public funding sources, community college administrators must develop policies and mechanisms for working with state and local governments to assure funding. Additionally, linkages with state level agencies in labor, social services, education, and economic development will prove fruitful in fiscal and programmatic areas. Senior administrators must identify and respond to issues important to legislators, commissioners and/or council members.

• The frameworks or coupling which allow community colleges to be active and successful in programming must reflect the differences in academic and non-academic programs. Vocational skill instruction, which is no longer the primary focus of most community colleges, must continue to have a role and be integrated into more traditional academic areas to enhance the nature of serving the college's local community.

• Community colleges may need to review the definition of departments, divisions, or areas. In addition to clarifying definitions, consideration should be given to the number and size of disciplines in a unit. Too often organizational structures are created out of organizational convenience rather than pedagogical affinity or commonality of mission. How different disciplines are combined into units can have an impact on faculty expectations, leadership style required, and student involvement and relationships.

• Community colleges may need to clarify the job descriptions of chair, head, coordinator/director, associate dean, etc. to eliminate any confusion which can lead to organizational stress, strife, and uncertainty of where job responsibilities begin and end. Role clarification is especially important to perceptions of expectations which if not clarified can influence the evaluation of performance by both faculty and upper administration.

PART II:

CHAIR PERCEPTIONS OF JOB DIMENSIONS

CHAPTER FOUR

Educational Beliefs and Values

What do community college chairs believe about their community college and the context in which they work? The department chair must be prepared to adapt to new and continually changing internal and external environments, and must also be capable of assisting faculty to adapt to new directions and environments. For example, community colleges are reexamining the place of comprehensive liberal education (Smutek, 1988) and the value and meaning of general education (Campbell, 1988). While leadership strategies may differ based on institutional context, the success of virtually all theories or strategies is focused on consensus building (Miller & Seagren, 1992). The identification, understanding, and commitment to a set of beliefs and values by the chair and all participants in the department are necessary if the chair is going to be effective in providing leadership to the department. This is especially true in community colleges because they are often viewed as being "all things to all people" (Eaton, 1992). However, limits of resources require the reexamination and focusing of mission.

There are currently several different perspectives concerning issues, trends, and perceptions of the mission and intent of formal education beyond the high school level. Faculty governance leaders, administrators at the various levels, part-time and full-time faculty, students, trustees, and business and industry leaders may have different views about the mission and purpose of postsecondary education. The department or unit head must not merely understand individual unit faculty perspectives toward beliefs and values, but must strive to comprehend the perspectives of the other actors and constituents who impact the unit. The chair must know how these individuals develop their beliefs and values toward certain issues and what strategies can be most effective if the beliefs and values need to be clarified or changed.

In addition, understanding one's own beliefs and values is vital to effective leadership. As Maehr and Braskamp (1986) argued in the context of motivation, only by first understanding and comprehending oneself can effective administrative practice be implemented. In order to cope with and thrive in the postsecondary context of change, the chairs must be aware of their own personal beliefs and values about current educational issues, particularly those dealing with the dimensions of the community college environment. Chairs were asked to complete the sentence: **"'I place a high value on _____' in terms of your current position for beliefs and value statements."**

What Chairs Said

As shown in **Table 4.1**, six beliefs and values were highly valued by more than 90% of the responding chairpersons. The six statements were reflective of traditional thinking within the realm of community colleges, as illustrated in Brint and Karabel's (1989) <u>Diverted Dream</u>. In this perspective, community colleges respond to constituent needs while promoting the ideals of continued or life-long learning. The highest rated statements were encouraging the use of a wide variety of teaching methods (96.8%), promoting life-long learning (96.1%), responding to community needs (94.1%), offering general education courses and programs (94.0%), responding to business and industry needs (92.8%), and providing student support services (90.3%).

At least 80% of the respondents rated as strongly agree or agree seven statements focused on instructional philosophy and instructional support. These statements were reflective of much of the work in student affairs and student development, ranging from notions of enhancing teaching and learning to providing remediation services. Statements included working to enroll more minority students (89.1%), concentrating on student knowledge through the use of a major (88.9%), offering occupational and technical education (88.7%), offering developmental courses for under-prepared students (86.4%), using computers in the classroom (85.3%), promoting and developing student leadership (83.4%), and serving the unique needs of at-risk student populations (80.6%).

At least 60% of the responding chairpersons agreed with the value of seven largely unrelated statements ranging from specific recommendations for courses to attitudes about student matriculation. The lack of cohesion in this group of statements may be reflective of Eaton's (1992) perspective noted earlier that many community colleges attempt to be all things to all constituents and, in the process, weaken their philosophical foundation. Statements in this group included students completing a degree program (79.3%), promoting values education (77.2%), open college admissions (77.0%), offering elective courses (74.9%), use of curriculum advisory committees (71.9%), offering English as a second language courses (65.1%), and open departmental admissions (60.2%). It is interesting to note that chairs believed in open access to the institution in greater numbers than in open access to their own departments. This reflects the concern, particularly in transfer programs, that students be appropriately prepared to perform at the community college and beyond (Roueche & Roueche, 1993).

Table 4.1: Frequency Table for Educational Beliefs and Values

Please indicate the extent of your agreement or disagreement with each of the following statements. Complete this sentence: "I place a high value on . . ." in terms of your current position in the unit.

Educational Beliefs and Values	Strongly Agree (1) or Agree (2)	Neutral (3)	Disagree (4) or Strongly Disagree (5)	Mean	Std. Dev.
The concept of life-long learning	96.1%	3.5%	0.4%	1.32	.57
Encouraging faculty to use a wide variety of teaching approaches	96.8	3.0	0.3	1.33	.55
General Education	94.0	4.6	1.3	1.41	.66
Preparing students to meet the needs of business/industry	92.8	6.0	1.2	1.48	.68
Preparing students to meet the needs of the community	94.1	5.3	0.6	1.50	.63
Occupational/technical education	88.7	8.9	2.4	1.56	.78
Promoting and encouraging the enrollment of minority students in the college	89.1	9.8	1.0	1.58	.72
Students gaining in-depth knowledge through a major	88.9	9.0	2.1	1.58	.76
Student support services	90.3	8.2	1.5	1.64	.70
Using computers in the classroom	85.3	12.8	1.7	1.71	.77
Providing development courses to students	86.4	9.6	4.0	1.72	.83
Opportunities for students to experience and understand leadership	83.4	15.0	1.5	1.81	.75

Table 4.1: Frequency Table for Educational Beliefs and Values (cont'd)

Educational Beliefs and Values	Strongly Agree (1) or Agree (2)	Neutral (3)	Disagree (4) or Strongly Disagree (5)	Mean	Std. Dev.
Students completing a degree program	79.3	16.7	4.0	1.85	.86
Serving at-risk students	80.6	16.3	3.0	1.89	.80
Values education incorporated into the curriculum	77.2	18.4	4.3	1.93	.87
An open admission policy for my college	77.0	10.2	12.7	1.96	1.11
Elective courses for students	74.9	21.0	4.0	2.02	.82
The role of an advisory committee in establishing the curriculum	71.9	18.8	9.3	2.13	.95
Offering courses for limited English speakers	65.1	25.0	9.9	2.24	.97
An open admission policy for my department	60.2	10.0	20.9	2.50	1.35
Training workers for specific companies	46.1	33.4	20.6	2.68	1.04
Limiting the influence of accreditation agencies	36.3	36.1	27.6	2.88	1.03
Courses designed with open entry/open exit	32.6	35.9	31.4	2.97	1.10
Having selective admissions policies	33.5	20.3	46.2	3.18	1.23

Ranked in order of importance by mean score
Legend: Strongly Agree = 1; Agree = 2; Neutral = 3; Disagree = 4; Strongly Disagree = 5

Less than 50% of the responding chairpersons rated as strongly agree or agree four statements scattered into several disparate areas of beliefs and values. All four show large standard deviations (over 1.0), demonstrating wide discrepancies in chair support for the statements. Statements in this group included training workers for business and industry (46.1%), limiting the influence of accrediting agencies (36.3%), having selective admissions policies and standards (33.5%), and promoting courses which have open entry and open exit policies (32.6%).

Beliefs and Values Clusters

As identified in **Table 4.2**, the statements of beliefs and values clustered together based on consistency in agreement rating using a factor analysis. Two clusters were generated: *beliefs about curriculum and students,* and *beliefs about mission and access.*

Table 4.2.   Beliefs and Values Clusters

Beliefs about Curriculum and Students

- Values education incorporated into the curriculum
- Opportunities for students to experience and understand leadership
- Using computers in the classroom
- Preparing students to meet the needs of the community
- Encouraging faculty to use a wide variety of teaching approaches
- Promoting and encouraging the enrollment of minority students in the college
- The concept of life-long learning
- Student support services
- Serving at-risk students
- Offering courses for limited English-speaking students
- Providing development courses to students

Beliefs about Mission and Access

- Occupational/technical education
- An open admission policy for my department (reverse code)
- An open admission policy for my college (reverse code)
- Preparing students to meet the needs of business/industry
- Having selective admissions policies
- The role of an advisory committee in establishing the curriculum

Beliefs about Curriculum and Students

The cluster of *beliefs about curriculum and students* included the following items: values education in curriculum, students experience and understanding of leadership, computer use in the classroom, preparing students for community needs, encouraging varied approaches to teaching, encouraging the enrollment of minority students, life-long learning, student support services, serving at-risk students, providing courses for limited English speakers, and providing developmental courses. The statements included in this cluster are consistent with the general philosophical underpinnings of community colleges. The curriculum needs to be flexible, focused on lifelong learning, developmental in approach, and include both values and leadership education. It is equally true that student support services are important because of the diversity of student needs.

Beliefs about Mission and Access

This second cluster included the following items: providing occupational and technical education, open departmental admissions and open college admissions (both reverse coded), providing preparation of students for business and industry needs, having selective admissions, and using advisory committees to establish a curriculum. It is clear the mission statements of community colleges generally include a provision for open admission (Roueche & Roueche, 1993). The use of advisory committees is also quite common for both the total campus and specific curriculum areas. This in turn provides input for enhancing the provision of occupational and technical education appropriate for business and industry needs.

These two clusters provide a conceptual framework with which to organize thinking about the varied beliefs and values of community college chairs. This framework has the potential to initiate a serious dialogue about both the reflection of these beliefs on the college's structures and the need to deal with the results of certain beliefs.

Summary

An understanding of chair beliefs and values toward selected educational issues provides implications for both leadership development and the policies and structures which support the chair position. Chairs had high levels of agreement for many of the educational beliefs and values identified but held especially strong levels of agreement for the value of six issues related to the commonly accepted role and mission of community colleges, and the factors which have driven their success.

These included: use of a wide variety of teaching methods, promoting life-long learning, responding to community needs, offering general education courses and programs, responding to business and industry needs, and providing student support services.

Implications for Leadership Development

• Chairs must become aware of the importance of and techniques used in promoting life-long learning. For instructional units to place a high value on continued learning, the chair must be prepared to offer guidance and direction on everything from curriculum to authentic assessment. Students must be provided with skills for life-long learning.

• Community colleges found initial success by using alternative teaching methods, and chairs must be aware of the appropriateness and advantages of different styles. In such a technology pervasive society, chairs will also want to explore the utilization of various technologies to enhance and improve teaching. Further, chairs must provide developmental activities for faculty to encourage the utilization of varied methods, and reward those who creatively and effectively meet student learning needs.

• Chairs placed a high value on general education, which means this topic should be included in leadership development to increase understanding and appreciation for liberal arts education. This should include attention to cultivating civic learning in students (Parnell, 1990). Chairs must create an environment where general education is seen as important.

• As students are prepared for business and industry and community needs, chairs must become knowledgeable of needs assessment techniques and procedures for evaluating and assessing the impact of the training provided. As a correlate to this, the chair must have the skills and be prepared to work in the external environment building relationships with business, industry, and community leaders.

• The instructional unit must be user-friendly, with the chair as the point person in addressing traditional student affairs issues. Chairs must believe that serving students is important, and be prepared to implement and encourage a variety of student-centered measures. Collaboration with and visits to institutions that have effective programs will enrich understanding of potential offerings and resources.

Implications for Policy and Campus Structure

• To more accurately meet the needs and accountability concerns of the community, business and industry, and students, advisory committees will increasingly prove to be helpful. The use of more advisory committees can subsequently impact curriculum, course scheduling, testing, and even instructional design.

• Incorporate the broader ideas of values and beliefs about community college education into the college's role, mission, and goal statements through strategic planning. At the department level, the chair should be prepared to include values and beliefs as components of the planning process. Institutions must encourage all members of the campus community to engage in continuing dialogue, draft position papers, and participate in retreats and ongoing committee work toward the end of shared responsibility and vision.

• Develop a reward system at the department level which gives greater attention to the student and student-related services. Encouragement and recognition by the chair of student centered activities like faculty-student mentoring can have an impact.

• Localize institutional student service programs at the department level. For the chair, this may include student orientation programming, teaching study skills, and offering pre-registration early advising.

• Develop a reward system which recognizes, at the department level, excellence and innovation in teaching. As a matter of policy, the chair may wish to offer mini-sabbaticals or mini-grants and intern opportunities for faculty to visit innovative programs, participate in conferences, read and think about how to reconceptualize how they teach.

• Determine whether student admission policies are specified, communicated to and understood by faculty, students, business and industry, and counselors in secondary schools. The importance of clearly spelling out standards can not be over emphasized. Faculty misunderstandings can result in unrealistic expectations (either high or low), leading to poor student performance or boredom. Students who don't have an appreciation of or rationale for standards may feel they are being treated unfairly. Business and industry representatives need to have input because they employ the graduates; if these individuals don't believe standards are appropriate or enforced, students will not be offered employment. Finally, counselors need to understand and interpret the standards to students who are making career choices. This is an important decision included in Boyer's (1987) seamless web concept.

CHAPTER FIVE

Roles

What are the typical roles that chairs assume in leading their instructional units? Organizations describe or in some cases even prescribe roles, a set of expectations, for those who have the responsibility for providing leadership. Academic chair roles in postsecondary education have been studied over the last 25 years (McLaughlin, Montgomery, & Malpass, 1975; Booth, 1982; Tucker, 1984; Creswell et al., 1990) with many roles continually surfacing (e.g., organizing, evaluating) and other roles occurring less frequently. Gmelch and Miskin (1993) identified four roles: faculty developer, manager, leader, scholar. A more traditional approach to the management function is Drucker's (1974) approach which identified planning, organizing, staffing, delegating and controlling as the main roles of administrators. After comparing the categories of roles identified among four-year to two-year institutions, Ferguson (1993) suggested that the complex role of the two-year chair involved budget and facilities, curriculum and articulation, personnel, and student relations issues. The successful acknowledgement and execution of all of these roles is crucial to getting the work of organizations accomplished.

From past literature about the typical roles of chairpersons, 14 frequently cited roles were presented to chairs to determine their perceived importance. The question asked was: **"How do you perceive your role as a chairperson? Indicate the degree of importance of each role to you in your current position."**

What Chairs Said

Given the complexity of the chair position, responses in **Table 5.1** suggest a picture of varying importance ascribed to different roles. Four roles: planner, information disseminator, motivator, and facilitator received 90% or more agreement among respondents as to importance. Fewer than 2% of all chairs suggested these roles were not important and only a small percentage, from 2.2-5.0%, were undecided. Since chairs have major responsibilities for organizing, keeping people informed, and creating an environment in which faculty and staff are motivated, this finding is not surprising. It is consistent with chair and management literature that suggests the importance of providing this leadership (Murray, 1992; Riggs & Akor, 1992). The finding is also consistent with Menschenfruend's (1993) research which concluded that the roles of motivator, planner, and facilitator were very important to community college deans.

Table 5.1: Frequency Table for Roles

How do you perceive your role as a chairperson? Indicate the degree of importance of each role to you in your current position:

Roles	Very Important (1) or Important (2)	Undecided (3)	Not Very Important (4) or Not Important (5)	Mean	Std. Dev.
Planner	97.4%	2.2%	0.4%	1.37	.55
Motivator	94.8	3.5	1.7	1.49	.66
Information disseminator	95.9	2.6	1.4	1.50	.63
Facilitator	93.4	5.0	1.6	1.60	.68
Advocate	89.1	8.7	2.2	1.68	.75
Visionary	89.3	7.0	3.7	1.71	.77
Conflict resolver	86.5	8.2	5.3	1.79	.84
Delegator	87.1	9.1	3.8	1.84	.76
Mentor	82.9	12.3	4.8	1.89	.83
Resource allocator	84.7	9.7	5.6	1.89	.83
Evaluator	82.5	11.2	6.3	1.95	.87
Negotiator	77.3	13.8	8.9	2.00	.96
Caretaker	55.0	25.2	19.9	2.52	1.0
Entrepreneur	45.1	29.5	25.5	2.73	1.2

Ranked in order of importance by mean score
Legend: Very Important = 1; Important = 2; Undecided = 3; Not Very Important = 4; Not Important = 5.

Seven roles, visionary, advocate, delegator, conflict resolver, resource allocator, mentor and evaluator, were perceived by 80% or more chairpersons as important. In addition, the negotiator role (77.3%) is close to this group. Once again these roles are consistently cited in the literature as crucial in establishing direction, addressing operations, and resolving frictions that sometimes arise in administering a department (Seagren, Creswell, & Wheeler, 1993). The visionary role was particularly noted by Roueche, Baker, and Rose (1989) in their work on transformational leaders as community college presidents; this same role can be practiced at the department level by chairs. A somewhat surprising finding was that 17.1% were undecided or disagreed with the importance of performing as a mentor. These chairs either were unaware they fill this role or they saw others as more suitable mentors. Responses from 22.7% of the chairs surveyed suggested that they were either neutral or perceived less importance of the negotiator role; yet only 13% were undecided or disagreed with the conflict resolver role. Negotiation may be perceived as a formal process associated with legalities, while the role of conflict resolver is more informal and part of the political nature of the position.

Fifty-five percent of the chairs rated the caretaker role as important. There was a standard deviation of 1.0, which suggests a greater variance of importance than previous roles identified. For this population of chairs, almost 20% did not see their role as maintenance of the status quo, and 25% were unsure of their role. The finding also suggests that chairs see themselves as leaders more than individuals responsible for "administrivia" in the unit (Creswell et al., 1990).

Less than 50% of the chairs suggested that the entrepreneur role was important. Of the chairs responding, 25.5% perceived this role as not important. At first this finding seems shocking, particularly given the autonomy of individual departments to engage with external constituents, but it may be a reflection that the entrepreneurial role is assumed by other administrators within the organization or by some other group on campus.

Role Clusters

The 14 roles grouped into clusters through a factor analysis, as shown in **Table 5.2**. Three major clusters emerged: *interpersonal role, administrator role,* and *leader role.*

Table 5.2. Role Clusters

Interpersonal Role
- Information disseminator
- Facilitator
- Mentor
- Advocate
- Caretaker

Table 5.2. Role Clusters (Cont'd)

Administrator Role
- Resource allocator
- Evaluator
- Negotiator
- Conflict resolver

Leader Role
- Visionary
- Motivator
- Entrepreneur
- Delegator
- Planner

Interpersonal Role

The roles in this cluster (i.e., information disseminator, facilitator, mentor, advocate, and caretaker) indicate its complexity. All are consistent with a need to be skilled in communication and the ability to relate with others. Many researchers (Tucker, 1984; Creswell et al., 1990) have indicated the importance of these roles and the negative consequences of the lack of attention to addressing relationships. As Murray (1992) indicated about community college chairs:

One respondent commented 'so much of being a department chair is like any other supervisory position; the biggest part of it is dealing with human beings and there is a lot of that you can't train for.' When asked to expand on what was meant by 'dealing with people,' the respondent said, 'an understanding of what is important to faculty— what the priorities are. . . .' (p. 12)

Principle-centered leadership, as advanced by Covey (1992) underlies some of these items, particularly with respect to the concept of interpersonal trust and its importance in information sharing and developing a work environment in which people strive to do well.

Administrator Role

The roles of resource allocator, evaluator, negotiator and conflict resolver comprise the *administrator role* cluster. These roles are logically related to one another as the chair is often expected to evaluate, determine resource allocations, and negotiate with faculty and staff. All of these roles require an ability to confront and work through potential differences with faculty and staff.

General chair literature (Tucker, 1984; Bennett & Frugili, 1990; Creswell et al., 1990) confirms the importance of these roles. One explanation for why this group was not perceived as more important is that, in some situations, there is not an expectation for the chair to assume responsibility because it rests with others at a higher administrative level. When the responsibility does rest with the chair, it presents a challenge for individuals who are uncomfortable in dealing with differing values and addressing the distribution of finite resources.

Leader Role

The *leader role* cluster is composed of the five roles: visionary, motivator, entrepreneur, delegator, and planner. All of these roles are central to moving a department forward. This cluster addresses the issue of what the vision can be (or will be in the future) as well as what roles are needed to implement the vision. If a department chair does not have all of the skills required for performing the roles in this cluster, others in the department can be identified to assume these roles and work with the department chair in a complementary and collaborative fashion. An assistant or associate chair is a popular model in especially large units (Creswell et al., 1990) and in at least one community college in Ohio, the chair position was split between two individuals (Murray, 1992).

These three clusters of roles are significant in the success of departmental chairing. Institutions should encourage all administrators to clarify which of these roles are to be emphasized and how other administrators are involved in providing guidance within the institution.

Summary

In summary, three-quarters or more of the chairs surveyed identified 12 roles as important. Two roles, the caretaker and entrepreneur, were rated with considerably less importance. The planner role was perceived to be the most important. This role underscores the importance of planning in community college departments, as noted by Riggs and Akor (1992) and Menschenfruend (1993). The priority of these roles has profound implications for academic leadership and institutional policy.

Implications for Leadership Development

Community college chairs can utilize the information gathered about the chair role and its most important aspects in several key ways:

• Design a range of professional development opportunities to increase effectiveness in all roles. These can include workshops and reading. Ongoing practicums with mentoring and journaling have also shown power in helping chairs reflect upon and grow in their decision making and understanding (Holly, 1984).

• Provide opportunities for chairs to discuss and explore planning issues. Case studies and simulations which balance time for planning against the demands of daily realities can be helpful. Research has shown that despite the importance ascribed to planning, it is given little attention compared to other administrative functions (Menschenfruend, 1993). The planning function is the one administrative function which can be ignored or not given high priority, but the organizational cost of doing so can be quite high over extended time periods.

• Chairs must accept feedback on, and work to perfect their facilitation and communication skills, especially those related to listening (Creswell et al., 1990). Student and faculty evaluations and dialogue are one means of identifying necessary information for growth in this area.

• Many of the roles (advocate, conflict resolver, mentor and evaluator) involve a set of intrapersonal and interpersonal skills. In surveys of chairs, dealing with conflict management is always high on the list. Assessment techniques, skill-building workshops and other opportunities are needed to perfect these skills in these roles.

• The visionary role is often difficult for chairs. Provide opportunities and encourage chairs to facilitate visioning in others. Senge (1990), Bennis and Nanus (1985), and Nanus (1992) provide some helpful ideas about collective and personal leadership visioning. For creating a departmental vision, also see the practical suggestions offered by Creswell et al. (1990) and Gmelch and Miskin (1993).

• Resource allocator and delegator require the ability to pull together what it takes (people, money, and responsibilities) to make plans work. Higher level administrators can provide coaching for chairs in this area. Creswell et al. (1990) found that how resources are allocated can have a powerful influence achieving priorities.

Implications for Policy and Campus Structure

The chair position is one of the most important leadership positions within the community college, and institutions can benefit from recognizing the importance of the varied roles that chairs assume when they undertake this position. Colleges should:

• Select chairs capable of performing well in the roles included in the interpersonal cluster.

• Expect that the greater the degree of departmental and individual change needed, the more important these roles become. Work with individuals making major career shifts suggests as much as five years may be necessary (see Lunde, Wheeler, Hartung, & Wheeler, 1991; Lunde & Hartung, 1990) to accomplish outcomes. Accomplishment of departmental goals often requires the same patience and extended timeframe.

• Assess the current status and effectiveness of chairs in all roles as an ongoing process, and expect concrete plans (short- and long-term) to address areas of importance.

• Encourage chairs to clarify and negotiate roles with faculty and upper administrators. Recent work by Seagren, Creswell, and Wheeler (1993) suggests a useful format to facilitate the process of role clarification. Menschenfruend (1993) found that chairs perceived the expectations of higher administrators in regard to roles were implied more often than explicitly spelled out.

• Use the clusters of roles as performance categories for chairs and their superiors and faculty to assess and develop on an ongoing basis.

CHAPTER SIX

Tasks

If chairs engage in specific roles as part of their job, what are the specific tasks that relate to these roles? Unquestionably, academic chairs occupy an important position in institutions of higher education. Roach (1976) estimated 80% of all university decisions are made at the departmental level. The importance of the chair was reinforced by Peltason (1984) when he noted that institutions can run a long time with inept presidents but not for long with inept chairpersons. Given these statements about importance, the next logical question is "what do and should chairs do?", or stated another way, "what are the important tasks chairs perform?" Numerous studies conducted about departmental chairs have given some attention to the range of tasks assigned or assumed by chairs. Seagren, Creswell, and Wheeler (1993) found at least 12 studies since 1965 that had attempted to map the roles, responsibilities, tasks, and duties, of chairs.

Several different approaches have been used to combine specific tasks into larger categories. Tucker (1992) collapsed 54 tasks into 28 roles and 7 responsibilities. Moses and Roe (1990) combined their list of functions into seven broad categories. The 32 tasks included in this study represented a consolidation and revision of those of Smart and Elton (1976); Seagren (1978); Jennerick (1981); McLaughlin, Montgomery, and Malpass (1975); Norton (1980); Moses and Roe (1990); and Tucker (1992).

Given the unique role of community colleges, some tasks unique to community college chairs were included. These tasks were designed to help clarify the profile of the chair position in community college but also provide insight into the topics to which should be included in academic leadership development programs and policy implications for community colleges. The community college chairs were asked to respond to the statement: **"Indicate the degree of importance of each task to you in your current position for each of the 32 tasks on a five-point scale, very important to not very important."**

What Chairs Said

The information in **Table 6.1** indicates a range of agreement as to importance of varied tasks from a high of 97.9% (communicate needs to upper level administration) to a low of 40.2% (seek external funding). More than 90% of the chairs believed in the importance of these 10 tasks: communicate needs to upper level administration (97.9%), create a positive work environment (97.5%), communicate information from administrators to unit faculty (95.5%), provide feedback to faculty (94.5%), recruit and select faculty (93.2%), update curriculum and courses (92.5%), encourage the professional development of each staff member (92%), set personal and professional goals (91.8%), develop long-range unit plans (91.2%), integrate unit plans with institutional plans (91.1%). These findings are not surprising, given the fact that most chairs have responsibility for planning; communicating to faculty departmentally and from upper administration; recruitment, selection and development of faculty; updating curriculum and course offerings; and creating a positive departmental culture.

Table 6.1: Frequency Table for Tasks

Below are listed tasks identified in the research literature as being performed by chairs or heads (or comparable position). Indicate the degree of importance of each task to you in your current position:

Tasks	Very Important (1) or Important (2)	Undecided (3)	Not Very Important (4) or Not Important (5)	Mean	Std. Dev.
Create a positive environment	97.5%	1.6%	0.8%	1.31	.56
Communicate needs to upper level administrators	97.9	1.3	0.7	1.32	.55
Recruit and select faculty	93.2	3.6	3.2	1.48	.76
Communicate information from administration to unit faculty	95.5	2.7	1.7	1.49	.66
Provide feedback to faculty	94.5	3.3	2.2	1.53	.71
Update curriculum and courses	92.5	4.1	3.4	1.58	.76
Encourage the professional development of each staff member	92.0	4.5	3.3	1.60	.76
Set personal and professional goals	91.8	4.7	3.4	1.62	.76
Develop long-range unit plans	91.2	5.7	3.1	1.63	.75
Schedule classes	88.9	4.1	7.1	1.64	.95

Table 6.1: Frequency Table for Tasks (cont'd)

Tasks	Very Important (1) or Important (2)	Undecided (3)	Not Very Important (4) or Not Important (5)	Mean	Std. Dev.
Integrate unit plans with institutional plans	91.1	5.9	3.0	1.69	.75
Prepare unit budgets	88.1	5.1	6.8	1.71	.93
Monitor unit budgets	88.4	5.3	6.4	1.73	.89
Assign faculty responsibilities	86.7	7.2	6.1	1.80	.88
Allocate resources to priority activities	85.2	8.0	6.9	1.81	.93
Evaluate faculty performance	84.9	8.1	7.1	1.82	.96
Conduct unit meetings	87.8	4.1	8.1	1.86	.87
Advise and counsel students	82.9	9.4	7.8	1.86	.94
Process paperwork and answer correspondence	84.9	9.0	6.1	1.90	.84
Prepare for accreditation	78.6	11.6	9.8	1.97	1.01
Promote affirmative action	75.3	14.8	9.9	2.06	1.03
Develop relationships with business and community groups	70.7	14.1	15.2	2.17	1.14
Supervise clerical/ technical staff	65.6	12.6	21.8	2.45	1.19
Manage facilities and equipment	69.0	12.7	18.3	2.32	1.13
Recruit students	58.6	17.6	23.7	2.49	1.23
Create unit committees	59.3	18.0	22.7	2.52	1.12
Develop clerical/technical staff	58.2	17.5	24.3	2.60	1.21
Help students register	57.9	13.5	28.6	2.62	1.29
Terminate faculty	54.3	19.5	26.2	2.65	1.29

Table 6.1: Frequency Table for Tasks (cont'd)

Tasks	Very Important (1) or Important (2)	Undecided (3)	Not Very Important (4) or Not Important (5)	Mean	Std. Dev.
Prepare enrollment projections	49.1	22.6	28.2	2.75	1.19
Maintain unit data bases	50.0	22.4	27.5	2.76	1.18
Seek external funding	40.2	22.1	37.6	3.02	1.29

Ranked in order of importance by mean score
Legend: Very Important = 1; Important = 2; Undecided = 3; Not Very
Important = 4; Not Important = 5

Another group of nine tasks were perceived by over 80% of the chairs as being important. Included in this group were: scheduling classes (88.9%), monitoring unit budget (88.4%), preparing unit budgets (88.1%), conducting unit meetings (87.8%), assigning faculty responsibilities (86.7%), allocating resources to priority activities (85.2%), evaluating faculty for performance (84.9%), process paper and answer correspondence (84.9%), and advise and counsel students (82.9%). The broad areas of budgeting, scheduling, faculty assignment, advising students, paper work, and conducting departmental meetings, all focus on activities that are much more routine and would tend to fall into Tucker's (1992) responsibilities of instruction, student affairs, budget and resources, and office management as well as in Gmelch and Miskin's (1993) manager role.

Five tasks were rated as important by more than two-thirds of the respondents: preparing for accreditation (78.6%), promoting affirmative action (75.3%), developing relationships with business and community groups (70.7%), managing facilities and equipment (69%), and supervising clerical/technical staff (66%). The tasks in this group were less specific and somewhat broader in nature, and each of the tasks could actually include a number of subtasks. For example, preparing for accreditation requires the preparation of historical data, the development of a statement of mission and goals, compilation of statistics about graduates, and the acquisition of library and computer resources. All of these tasks had a standard deviation greater than 1.0, indicating considerable variation in terms of importance.

There were six tasks for which slightly over one-half of the chairs indicated responses of very important or important. Creating unit committees (59.3%), recruiting students (58.6%), develop clerical/technical staff (58.2%), help students register (57.9%), terminate faculty (54.3%), and maintain unit databases (50%). Several tasks in this group might have been rated lower in terms of importance because they are the primary responsibility of another individual or office within the institution. The standard deviation for all of these tasks was greater than one, indicating considerable variation in terms of perceived importance.

Finally, two tasks, prepare enrollment projections (49.1%), and seek external funding (40.2%) were rated by less than 50% of the chairs as being very important or important. These results are not surprising, given the fact that the preparation of enrollment projections is often the responsibility of another office, such as admissions, planning, or institutional research. In a similar fashion, the task of seeking external funding is often a part of the responsibility of the campus president or the system chancellor or a specific development officer. This lack of interest in seeking external support is also consistent with the low ranking given the role of entrepreneur (see Chapter Five). The standard deviation was greater than 1.2 for both items, indicating a great deal of variation in terms of importance.

Task Clusters

Through factor analysis, the tasks grouped into seven clusters as shown in **Table 6.2**. Each cluster included from three to six tasks.

Table 6.2. Task Clusters

Professional Development and Communication Tasks
- Create a positive work environment
- Communicate needs to upper-level administrators
- Set personal and professional goals
- Encourage the professional development of each faculty member
- Promote affirmative action
- Communicate information from administration to unit faculty

Table 6.2 Task Clusters (Cont'd)

Faculty Selection & Feedback Tasks
- Recruit and select faculty
- Assign faculty responsibilities
- Evaluate faculty performance
- Provide feedback to faculty
- Terminate faculty

Budget Tasks
- Prepare unit budgets
- Monitor unit budgets
- Allocate resources to priority activities

Internal Tasks
- Supervise clerical/technical staff
- Maintain unit data bases
- Manage facilities and equipment
- Develop clerical/technical staff
- Prepare enrollment projections
- Process paperwork and answer correspondence

External Tasks
- Recruit students
- Develop relationships with business and community groups
- Seek external funding

Curriculum and Student Tasks
- Schedule classes
- Update curriculum and courses
- Advise and counsel students
- Help students register

Planning Tasks
- Integrate unit plans with institutional plans
- Conduct unit meetings
- Create unit committees
- Develop long-range unit plans
- Prepare for accreditation

Professional Development and Communication Tasks

The *professional development and communication tasks* cluster is composed of the tasks: create a positive environment, communicate to upper level administrators, set personal and professional goals, encourage faculty development, promote affirmative action, and communicate from administration to faculty. All of these tasks are consistent with the literature as found in Creswell et al. (1990). These findings are connected with Tucker's (1992) list of responsibilities in external communication, faculty affairs, departmental governance, and professional development. They also underscore the importance of information flowing downward, laterally, and upward between chairs and others in the organization (Stacks & Hickson, 1992). These findings also highlight the need for chairs to have the capacity for transformational leadership, which moves faculty beyond their basic needs to higher levels of commitment and fulfillment (Bass, 1985).

Faculty Selection and Feedback Tasks

The *faculty selection and feedback tasks* cluster involved five items: recruit/ select faculty, assign faculty responsibilities, evaluate faculty performance, provide feedback to faculty, and terminate faculty. These tasks are consistent with Tucker's (1992) lists of responsibilities under the broad heading of faculty affairs and are emphasized in Scott's (1990) findings about the faculty development role of community college chairs.

Budget Tasks

The *budget tasks* cluster involved three broad tasks: prepare unit budgets, monitor unit budgets, and allocate resources. The department is usually the lowest level considered as a cost center, and the responsibility for administering the budget is a major one for the chair in most institutions. Creswell et al. (1990) found that how the budget is managed and the degree of openness in that process can either help create an open trusting atmosphere in the department or the converse; the authors also determined the process for allocating resources can be powerful one in terms of reinforcing program and departmental priorities.

Internal Tasks

The *internal tasks* cluster included six items: supervise clerical/technical staff, maintain unit databases, manage facilities and equipment, develop clerical/technical staff, prepare enrollment projections, and process paper work. Studies of departmental chairs have indicated that these tasks are among the most disliked, and which provide the least amount of satisfaction for chairs (Tucker, 1984). However, Creswell et al. (1990) found that how efficiently these tasks are performed by the chair can contribute to how faculty and staff feel about the department and how positively the culture is viewed by them. They also found that most administrators would like to eliminate paper work. Chairs who were efficient at handling paperwork delegated as much as possible of the routine to office/clerical staff and attempted to only handle a piece of paper once.

External Tasks

The *external tasks* cluster is composed of three tasks: recruiting students, developing relationships with business and community, and seeking external funding. These three tasks do not appear to be closely related. However, when combined they communicate a vision of the department to external constituents. The importance of these tasks may be impacted by the discipline or subject area. For example, a department associated with an academic transfer program may not place the same degree of importance on some of the particular tasks in this cluster as one of the more vocational or technically oriented programs. A department of English does not have the same concern or opportunity to seek external funding as a department related to business administration and accounting. Relationships with business and industry were not included in Tucker's (1992) list of responsibilities nor specifically mentioned by Gmelch and Miskin (1993), however, the development of relationships with business and industry has long been a function of community colleges and as such is an area in need of further explanation. Menschenfruend (1993) found that upper administrators saw developing relationships with business and industry and seeking external funding as chair tasks that should be given greater attention.

Curriculum and Student Tasks

The *curriculum and student tasks* cluster is composed of four tasks, schedule classes, update curriculum/courses, advise/counsel students, and help students register. The three thrusts that exist in this cluster relate to curriculum, scheduling, and students. These tasks are at the heart of most educational organizations and institutions. How well students are advised and counseled about the courses for which they should register can determine to a large extent how successful students will be in terms of grades, and more importantly in the job market. On the other

65

hand, if the curriculum is not kept up to date students will not be well prepared to meet the needs of business and industry or the requirements of transfer programs. Scheduling of courses is important because course schedules need to accommodate the needs of students. This factor is especially important because of the nature of the student body. There are large numbers of part-time students and many full-time students, both of whom have heavy or full-time work schedules, enrolled in community colleges, and these individuals require class schedules which will accommodate work schedules.

Planning Tasks

The *planning tasks* cluster involves five tasks: integrate unit plans with institutional plans, conduct unit meetings, create unit committees, develop long-range plans, and prepare for accreditation. Two of these tasks relate directly to the planning function, first planning for the department alone and secondly integrating these plans with institutional plans. Chairs play a key role in keeping these two in perspective and in balance. It is easy for the faculty to become discouraged if departmental plans are not recognized and incorporated into institutional plans or if departmental goals/plans do not reflect institutional direction and reward systems.

The remaining three tasks support planning but can also be related to the operation of the department. The chair is in a key position to provide leadership and influence how effectively the committee structure of a department will function. For example, McNulty (1980) recorded five approaches leaders of university committees could take to enhance the proficiency of committee members: (a) evaluate group meeting process, (b) utilize a variety of group leadership skills, (c) utilize controlled group process methods, (d) systematically obtain feedback on the extent of decision making effort, and (e) clarify tasks assignments. These provide a useful framework for the chair to use with department committees. Moreover, a skilled chair must acquire a high degree of competence in the strategies and tactics of impression management, agenda setting, networking, and negotiations (Seagren, Creswell, & Wheeler 1993).

The chair must possess skill in creating and utilizing the results of committee efforts. In addition the manner in which unit meetings are conducted contributes to developing a sense of community and teaming, or the opposite. This thought echoes the importance, being discussed nationally in the postsecondary education community, of individuals feeling part of a community and having a sense of membership and belongingness (Boyer, 1987; Palmer, Wheeler, & Fowler, 1990). To do this, chairs need to be skillful in group dynamics, and capable of recognizing the myriad roles that faculty may play (e.g., facilitator, evaluator, blocker, or leader).

Summary

Over half of the 32 tasks presented (n = 19) were perceived as very important or important by over 80% of the chairs surveyed. These tasks were focused on communication; faculty recruitment/selection, professional development, assignment, and evaluation and feedback; creating a positive work environment; keeping the curriculum and courses updated and scheduling classes; setting personal and professional goals; developing unit plans and integrating these into institutional plans; preparing and monitoring the budget, and allocating resources; conducting departmental meetings; advising and counseling students; and processing paper work. The range of tasks important to community college chairs is surprisingly consistent with those identified in previous studies of tasks important to chairs in four-year institutions (Tucker, 1992; Seagren, Creswell, & Wheeler, 1993). Chairs assuming responsibility for this range of tasks also reinforces the importance of chairs as being a key or point person in the department and the institution in terms of faculty, instructional program, planning, budgeting, and students.

Implications for Leadership Development

The implications of these data related to the importance of tasks for leadership development suggest the following topics should be given high priority:

• Procedures and process for the development of unit strategies and operational plans and skill in integrating the unit and institutional plans.

• Communication and interpersonal skills, including those related and important to creating a positive work environment, facilitating effective department meetings, and encouraging productive committee work, and the practice of transformational leadership.

• Procedures for faculty recruitment, selection, development, assignment and evaluation. Each of these major types need to be presented in detail and a review of existing models or approaches provided with opportunities for development of procedures which are appropriate for the institution.

• Fiscal management: budget preparation and monitoring and resource allocation.

• Curriculum and course updating, and class scheduling.

• Student advising and counseling.

• Paper work and time management.

Depending upon the size of the institution, the other resources available to the institution, the degree of centralization or decentralization, and the job description of the chair, the following topics may need to be included in leadership development:

- Accreditation reports and preparation.
- Affirmative action procedures.
- Business and industry relationships.
- Clerical staff supervision and development.
- Physical facilities management.

Thus, the leadership development program, to a considerable degree, must be individualized and designed with consideration given to chair needs, the situation in the department, and the institutional context. These data also indicate the importance of conducting a needs assessment either locally or regionally to identify those topics most relevant to the group of chairs prior to designing and finalizing the specific topics to be included in the academic leadership development program. Such a process also helps to build ownership on the part of participants.

Implications for Policy and Campus Structure

There are also a number of policy implications which need to be considered based on these findings for community colleges. Institutional leaders must ask the following questions and take appropriate action if the response is negative:

- Are the procedures for integrating academic unit plans with the institutional plan specified in policy? If procedures are not in place and understood, it is easy for faculty to become over-ambitious and unrealistic in their planning efforts, then to become discouraged when the plans they have spent considerable time in developing are ignored.
- Are the processes, procedures, and policies for curriculum and course approval clearly specified for the chair and the department? Curriculum and course planning is at the heart of most programs, and guidance is needed to assure the content is kept up to date, evaluated continuously and relevant to student needs.
- Are the policies related to faculty recruitment, selection, appointment, assignment, development and evaluation current, comprehensive and consistent with Federal Affirmative Action guidelines and effective human resource management standards? If not, a range of legal action can result which can be costly in terms of dollars and human resources.
- Are the budget guidelines developed with appropriate input from faculty, chairs, deans, and other administrators, and do they provide guidance to the chair for supervising and monitoring the budget? As Creswell et al. (1990) found, the manner and the degree of openness with which the budget is managed contributes

to the degree of trust which exists in the unit. Trust then becomes an important factor in determining the unit culture. Openness encourages faculty to be realistic about the financial situation and to strategize for how to get the most out of the dollars to meet crucial needs. On the other hand, if faculty believe they are being treated unfairly by the chair, a negative back-stabbing culture can develop. Bowen (1980) says institutions of higher education are spending institutions—and there is never enough money to meet all needs. Secrecy about the amount of money available in the unit, and how much each individual faculty member receives, can only lead to a lack of trust on the part of faculty and a lack of cohesion within the unit.

CHAPTER SEVEN

Skills

What skills are needed by chairs to carry out their tasks and roles? A variety of skills have been identified as important in working in the context of the community college. Indeed, the future of the community college is confronted with the range of issues facing higher education (Hawthorne & Ninke, 1990) and secondary schools (Sirotnik & Goodlad, 1988); these include issues of collaboration and partnerships, as well as faculty renewal (Brass, 1984; El-Khawas, 1991). Chairs in particular must be capable of effectively and efficiently utilizing a number of skills that will enable them to communicate with faculty and upper-level administrators and provide leadership in a manner which will allow the opportunity for continued interaction as an equal with their faculty co-workers (Seagren, Creswell, & Wheeler, 1993). Chairs were asked to rate the importance of 12 statements which have been identified as crucial to effective administration in school settings adapted from the National Association of Secondary School Principals' Assessment Center Project. The question was asked: **"How important are these skills to you in your present position as a chair or head?"**

What Chairs Said

As shown in **Table 7.1**, respondents agreed that nearly all of the skills identified were important. Virtually every respondent indicated that three skills in particular were crucial. These included sensitivity: the ability to deal effectively with people (99.3%); judgement: the ability to reach logical conclusions and make high quality decisions (99.0%); and written communication: the ability to express ideas clearly in writing (99.0%).

Seven statements were rated by 96% or more of the responding chairs as important. These statements of skill included organizational ability: the ability to be organized in dealing with a volume of paper work and heavy demands on one's time (98.8%); leadership: the ability to recognize when a group required direction (98.7%); decisiveness: the ability to recognize when a decision is required (98.5%); oral communication: the ability to make a clear oral presentation (98.5%); educational values: the ability to be receptive to new ideas and change (98.0%); stress tolerance: the ability to perform under pressure (97.7%); and problem analysis: the ability to seek out data and information to solve a problem (96.6%).

Table 7.1: Frequency Table for Skills

Below are listed skills. How important are these skills to you in your present position as chair or head (or comparable position)?

Skills	Very Important (1) or Important (2)	Undecided (3)	Not Very Important (4) or Not Important (5)	Mean	Std. Dev.
Sensitivity: Ability to deal effectively with people	99.3%	.6%	0.1%	1.21	.43
Judgment: Ability to reach logical conclusions and make high quality decisions	99.0	.6	0.4	1.21	.46
Organizational ability: Ability to be organized in dealing with a volume of paperwork and heavy demands on one's time	98.8	.7	0.5	1.26	.49
Leadership: Ability to recognize when a group requires direction	98.7	.9	0.4	1.27	.50
Decisiveness: Ability to recognize when a decision is required	98.5	1.2	0.3	1.28	.50
Written communication: Ability to express ideas clearly in writing	99.0	.8	0.2	1.31	.50
Oral communication: Ability to make a clear oral presentation	98.5	1.2	0.3	1.33	.52
Stress tolerance: Ability to perform under pressure	97.7	1.7	0.6	1.33	.55

Table 7.1: Frequency Table for Skills (Cont'd)

Skills	Very Important (1) or Important (2)	Undecided (3)	Not Very Important (4) or Not Important (5)	Mean	Std. Dev.
Educational values: Ability to be receptive to new ideas and change	98.0	1.4	0.6	1.33	.54
Problem analysis: Ability to seek out data and information to solve a problem	96.8	1.7	1.5	1.37	.62
Personal motivation: Ability to show a need to achieve	83.9	10.6	5.6	1.82	.86
Range of interests: Ability to discuss a variety of societal issues	74.1	15.6	10.2	2.11	.93

Ranked in order of importance by mean score
Legend: Very Important = 1; Important = 2; Undecided = 3; Not Very
Important = 4; Not Important = 5.

The final two statements, rated by fewer chairs as important, included personal motivation: the ability to show a need to achieve, which was rated as very important or important by 83.9% of the respondents; and, range of interests: the ability to discuss a variety of societal issues, which was rated with importance by 74.1% of the respondents.

Skill Clusters

As reported in Table 7.2, the 12 skills were clustered into groups which reflected consistency in responses.

Table 7.2. Skill Clusters

Administrative Skills and Leadership
- Problem analysis: Ability to seek out data and information to solve a problem
- Judgement: Ability to reach logical conclusions and make high quality decisions
- Organizational ability: Ability to be organized in dealing with a volume of paperwork and heavy demands on one's time
- Decisiveness: Ability to recognize when a decision is required
- Leadership: Ability to recognize when a group requires direction

Interpersonal Skills
- Sensitivity: Ability to deal effectively with people
- Stress tolerance: Ability to perform under pressure
- Oral communication: Ability to make a clear oral presentation
- Written communication: Ability to express ideas clearly in writing

Individual Skills
- Range of interests: Ability to discuss a variety of societal issues
- Personal motivation: Ability to show a need to achieve
- Educational values: Ability to be receptive to new ideas and change

Administrative Skills and Leadership

The first cluster of statements dealt with *administrative skills and leadership*, and included the skills of problem analysis, judgement, organizational ability, decisiveness, and leadership. This cluster seemed indicative of the business operations of the unit such as budgeting, planning, and personnel supervision. In particular, the cluster represented the need of the chair to have the skills necessary to deal with the day-to-day operations of serving the needs of the faculty and upper-level administration.

Interpersonal Skills

The second cluster of statements dealt with *interpersonal skills*, and included sensitivity, stress tolerance, oral communication, and written communication. These skills relate primarily to the internal management of human resources. As noted in previous chapters, however, there is an increasing need for the chair to possess these skills as they relate to external constituencies such as accrediting bodies, business and industry, foundations and other potential funding sources, and advisory committees.

Individual Skills

The final cluster of skills dealt with *individual skills*, and included range of interests, personal motivation, and educational values. These skills may be considered the most important to the personal and professional longevity of the chair. A strong cadre of skills in this area provide the chair with an ability to reach a fulfilling balance between work and personal life.

Summary

Chairs overwhelmingly felt that all of the skills identified were important to their work. Given this group of chairs had an average of 6-10 years of experience, it appears safe to assume they have recognized the impact that the effective use of these skills can have on the department. In particular, chairs felt the most important skills dealt with the management of human resources (sensitivity and written communication skills) and individual judgement. This finding is not surprising, given the fact the list of skills has been developed and refined over a period of time by the NASSP Assessment Center project. Evidence for this project clearly demonstrates the ability of a principal to perform these skills effectively has an impact on the quality of leadership provided. Why data does not exist for testing this same dynamic for community college chairs is not clear.

Implications for Leadership Development

The implications of these data related to the importance of these skills for leadership development suggest consideration must be given to the following:
• Incorporate training on all of the skills into programs for community college chairs and academic leaders.
• Explore adapting the material and strategies utilized in the National Association of Secondary School Principals Assessment Center project so they are appropriate for community college chairs.
• Design and develop case studies, critical incidents or other types of simulations which would provide opportunities for chairs to demonstrate competency in the

imitation and use of these skills. Such simulations would provide opportunities for practice, feedback, and assessment of performance.

• Design extended practicums which would present opportunities for practice, feedback, and assessment cycle to be repeated a number of times for each of the skills. Such a practice would facilitate monitoring with the opportunity for providing feedback to participants.

Implications for Policy and Campus Structure

There are several policy implications for this area even though development on each of these skills needs to be individualized based on chair needs, departmental selection and institutional control.

• Current chairs and other administrators must develop a system for identifying future chairs. The skill areas identified here can suggest a framework for chair pre-service training. Public schools, for example, have found such models of leadership development helpful in identifying a pool of individuals who are available when leadership opportunities arise and positions become available.

• Institutions should adopt a policy of appointing chairs only after appropriate skill assessment and leadership training have occurred.

• Institutions must support the professional and institutional networking of chairs, which can be an effective approach to skill development and has tremendous implications for institutional health.

CHAPTER EIGHT

Job Challenges

What challenges, both within and external to the department or division, do chairs face as they engage in roles, tasks, and skills? Challenges facing department chairs are in large part determined by the roles chairs accept. If one tends to focus on maintaining the status quo, then challenges may be short-term and limited in scope. Conversely, if one views oneself as a visionary (Riggs & Akor, 1992), challenges may be longer term in nature and broader in scope. What is perceived as important by the individual will shape the future of the department, so responsibility for these challenges should be clarified.

From an analysis of the leadership literature, 33 job challenges were presented to chairs to determine their perceived importance. The question asked was: **"To what extent do you agree that the following are challenges you will have to face in your unit in the next five years?"**

What Chairs Said

Responses in **Table 8.1** indicate a wide range of agreement among surveyed chairs, from a high of 97.3% (maintaining program quality) to a low of 19.3% (decreasing growth in transfer programs). Four challenges were perceived as being important issues faced by 90% or more of the chairs: maintaining program quality (97.3%), maintaining high quality faculty (95.4%), strengthening curriculum (94.0%), and changing the curriculum in response to technological development (90.6%). These highest rated items are focused on program and faculty quality, and strengthening the curriculum, and likely reflect the recent intense emphasis on quality within the organizational development literature (see Chaffee & Sherr, 1991; Seymour, 1993). Also influencing the importance of these challenges is the increasing influence of accreditation agencies and potential employers who expect a curriculum that prepares students for an ever-complex world.

Table 8.1: Frequency Table for Challenges

To what extent do you agree that the following are challenges you will have to face in your unit in the next five years:

Challenges	Strongly Agree (1) or Agree (2)	Neutral (3)	Disagree (4) or Strongly Disagree (5)	Mean	Std. Dev.
Maintaining program quality	97.3%	1.8%	0.8%	1.32	.56
Maintaining a high quality faculty	95.4	2.7	1.9	1.37	.65
Strengthening the curriculum	94.0	4.9	1.2	1.47	.65
Changing the curriculum in response to technological development	90.6	6.5	3.0	1.51	.77
Responding to the needs of a wider range of students	88.6	8.4	3.0	1.69	.76
Securing and maintaining state-of-the-art technical equipment	85.3	9.9	4.9	1.73	.88
Increasing the use of computers in the classroom	87.0	9.3	3.8	1.74	.82
Employing new teaching techniques	89.0	9.1	1.9	1.74	.71
Keeping pace with the increasing cost of technology	84.5	11.0	4.4	1.79	.85
Obtaining financial resources	81.1	12.3	6.7	1.84	.96
Addressing accountability issues	80.6	15.3	4.1	1.94	.83
Reallocating monies to programs because of financial constraints	77.3	16.1	6.6	1.96	.93
Serving at-risk students	74.1	20.5	5.5	2.04	.88
Attracting new student populations	73.2	18.4	8.3	2.06	.95
Identifying unit leadership potential from among the faculty	75.7	17.4	6.9	2.06	.89

Table 8.1: Frequency Table for Challenges (Cont'd)

Challenges	Strongly Agree (1) or Agree (2)	Neutral (3)	Disagree (4) or Strongly Disagree (5)	Mean	Std. Dev.
Providing leadership training for faculty and chairs	71.6	19.7	8.7	2.10	.98
Accommodating cultural diversity	72.1	19.5	8.3	2.10	.98
Developing efficient advisory and registration systems and procedures	72.3	17.3	10.3	2.11	1.02
Utilizing more faculty development techniques such as classroom assessment, peer coaching, etc.	71.3	22.4	6.2	2.12	.88
Maintaining the physical plant	66.5	17.6	15.9	2.27	1.17
Addressing the issues of training for senior faculty	63.3	25.3	11.4	2.29	1.01
Increasing human relations training	61.6	27.3	11.1	2.32	.94
Promoting greater gender equity	59.5	27.2	13.3	2.35	1.03
Using quality management techniques (e.g., TQM)	58.6	29.8	11.6	2.35	1.03
Encouraging more technical preparation in high schools	59.6	24.3	16.0	2.36	1.12
Increasing emphasis on the transfer program	57.6	30.5	11.8	2.38	.98
Increasing the use of business and industry advisory committees	58.5	26.1	15.5	2.41	1.07
Increasing the general education requirements	54.4	26.1	19.4	2.49	1.05
Increasing influence and impact of state coordinating bodies	54.0	28.2	17.9	2.50	1.10

Table 8.1: Frequency Table for Challenges (Cont'd)

Challenges	Strongly Agree (1) or Agree (2)	Neutral (3)	Disagree (4) or Strongly Disagree (5)	Mean	Std. Dev.
Offering courses through distance education	51.3	28.9	19.8	2.57	1.11
Increasing influence and impact of accrediting bodies	45.2	33.9	20.9	2.67	1.05
Internationalizing the curriculum	41.8	32.6	25.5	2.79	1.08
Increasing teaching programs sponsored by specific companies	38.9	36.4	24.7	2.83	1.06
Adapting to employees who utilize electronic communication systems and who work at home	32.7	35.2	32.1	3.02	1.11
Increasing involvement of the U.S. Government in establishing work conditions in colleges	21.0	36.6	42.4	3.33	1.11
Decreasing growth in transfer programs	19.3	31.2	49.5	3.42	1.09

Ranked in order of importance by mean score
Legend: Strongly Agree = 1; Agree = 2; Neutral = 3; Disagree = 4; Strongly
Disagree = 5.

Over 80% of the chairs agreed on the importance of seven other challenges in the next five years. Included are: employing new teaching techniques (89.0%), responding to the needs of a wider range of students (88.6%), increasing the use of computers in the classroom (87.0%), securing and maintaining state-of-the-art equipment (85.3%), keeping pace with the increasing cost of technology (84.5%), obtaining financial resources (81.1%), and addressing accountability issues (80.6%). Consistent with the Carnegie Foundation for the Advancement of Teaching (1989) survey and reinforcing the findings in Chapter Two, these results confirm faculty in community colleges have a strong commitment to teaching issues. Certainly the closeness of community colleges to the technological orientation in businesses reinforces the necessity of keeping the curriculum relevant to the "real world."

Eight challenges were identified as challenges by 70% or more of the chairs. These include: reallocating monies to programs because of financial constraints (77.3%), identifying unit leadership potential from among the faculty (75.7%), serving at-risk students (74.1%), attracting new student populations (73.2%), developing efficient advisory and registration systems and procedures (72.3%), accommodating cultural diversity (72.1%), providing leadership training for faculty and chairs (71.6%), and utilizing more faculty development techniques such as assessment, peer coaching, etc. (71.3%). Given the necessity and inclination of community colleges to make adjustments to be responsive to the environment, these challenges focusing upon recruitment and retention of students, as well as faculty development and leadership, are consistent with these expectations. A number of these challenges show standard deviations near 1.0, as over 20% of the chairs are either neutral or disagree with their importance. Different institutional expectations may account for these differences.

Four challenges, maintaining the physical plant (66.5%), addressing issues of training for senior faculty (63.3%), increasing human relations training (61.6%), and encouraging more technical preparation in high schools (61.3%) were identified as important by 60% or more chairs. However, three of these four challenges have standard deviations of 1.0 or greater; more than 30% of the chairs disagreed or were neutral about the importance of these challenges. Two of these challenges, senior faculty training and human relations training, address crucial faculty development needs (see Boice, 1992; Creswell et al., 1990). One might expect more agreement about these challenges given an aging faculty and the importance placed on relationships with others as illustrated in the Roles, Tasks, and Skills Chapters (6,7,8). Several factors may explain chairs' relative lack of concern regarding maintenance of the physical plant. First, not providing for deferred maintenance is common in postsecondary education. Second, many community college facilities are relatively new, requiring little long-range maintenance. Finally, maintaining physical facilities in many institutions may be a responsibility of a higher-level administrative unit or be assigned to physical plant operations. The variation among responses to the item regarding encouraging greater high school tech preparation is predictable, given the range of institutional expectations and student preparation.

Seven challenges were perceived as important by 50% or more of the chairs: promoting greater gender equity (59.5%), using quality management techniques (e.g., Total Quality Management) (58.6%), increasing the use of business and industry advisory committees (58.5%), increasing emphasis on the transfer program (57.6%), increasing general education requirements (54.4%), increasing influence and impact of state coordinating bodies (54.0%), and offering courses through distance education (51.3%). All but one had standard deviations of 1.0 or more, indicating considerable variation in agreement. Some of these challenges (gender equity and general education) are perceived as somewhat controversial or wide-ranging in terms of expectations. Other challenges, such as advisory committees and state coordinating bodies, may not be perceived as important because institutions may already have structures, procedures, and activities in place which are meeting expectations; distance education may not seem as significant to these institutions due to their regional/local focus.

Four challenges, increasing influence and impact of accrediting bodies (45.2%), internationalizing the curriculum (41.8%), increasing teaching programs sponsored by specific companies (38.9%), adapting to employees who utilize electronic communication systems and who work at home (32.7%), were suggested as important challenges by one-third to one-half of the chairs. Again, all of these challenges have standard deviations of 1.0 or more indicating considerable variation in agreement. One might expect internationalizing the curriculum to be perceived as more of a challenge. Possible explanations are that many institutions believe they already have a curriculum and international experiences in place, or since the community college mission is focused on local needs, this dimension is not important. Internationalizing the curriculum is receiving increased attention, however, through linkages such as those developed by the College and University Partnership (CUP) program working with the Japan Foundation and the Global Networking Project. The same situation related to having intact structures, procedures and programs may be true with accrediting bodies and company-sponsored teaching. Employees working at home may be a challenge beyond the scope of many institutions; possibly in future years this will become a more important issue.

The lowest rated challenges by chairs were increasing involvement of the United States government in establishing working conditions in colleges (21.0%), and decreasing growth in transfer programs (19.3%). With standard deviations of over 1.0 and over 70% of respondents disagreeing with their importance, these challenges show the greatest variation and least support. The national shift toward academic transfer, with community colleges as feeder schools is gaining acceptance. Chairs may see no need to intervene against market forces to decrease this growth.

Challenge Clusters

Through a factor analysis, challenges grouped into nine clusters based upon similarities in responses (as shown in **Table 8.2**). Each cluster is composed of three to six challenges.

Table 8.2. Challenge Clusters

Faculty Challenges
- Addressing issues of training for senior faculty
- Employing new teaching techniques
- Identifying unit leadership potential from among the faculty
- Providing leadership training for faculty and chairs
- Utilizing more faculty development techniques such as classroom assessment, peer coaching, etc.

Student Challenges
- Offering courses through distance education
- Promoting greater gender equity
- Accommodating cultural diversity
- Responding to the needs of a wider range of students
- Serving at-risk students
- Attracting new student populations

External Relations Challenges
- Decreasing growth in transfer programs
- Encouraging more technical preparation in high schools committees
- Increasing teaching programs sponsored by specific companies
- Adapting to employees who utilize electronic communication systems and who work at home

Technology Challenges
- Changing the curriculum in response to technological development
- Keeping pace with the increasing cost of technology
- Securing and maintaining state-of-the-art technical equipment
- Increasing the use of computers in classroom

Program Quality Challenges
- Maintaining program quality
- Strengthening the curriculum
- Maintaining a high quality faculty

Table 8.2. Challenge Clusters (Cont'd)

External Accountability Challenges
- Increasing influence and impact of state coordinating bodies
- Increasing influence and impact of accrediting bodies
- Increasing involvement of the U.S. Government in establishing work conditions in colleges

Financial Resources Challenges
- Obtaining financial resources
- Maintaining the physical plant
- Reallocating monies to programs because of financial constraints

Curriculum Challenges
- Increasing general education requirements
- Increasing human relations training
- Internationalizing the curriculum
- Increasing emphasis on the transfer program

Internal Accountability Challenges
- Using quality management techniques (e.g., TQM)
- Addressing accountability issues
- Developing efficient advisory and registration systems and procedures

Faculty Challenges

The *faculty challenges* cluster is composed of: addressing issues of training for senior faculty, employing new teaching techniques, identifying unit leadership potential from among the faculty, providing leadership training for faculty and chairs, and utilizing more faculty development techniques such as classroom assessment, peer coaching, etc. All of these challenges fit well with the literature (Tucker, 1984; Eble, 1986; Creswell et al., 1990) that suggests the key role that chairs play in providing help and support for faculty to address present and prepare for future needs.

Student Challenges

Student challenges include: offering courses through distance education, promoting greater gender equity, accommodating cultural diversity, responding to the needs of a wider range of students, serving at-risk students, and attracting new student populations. This cluster is focused on various student challenges all related to instruction—the historical backbone of community colleges.

External Relations Challenges

The *external relations challenges* cluster involves five items: decreasing growth in transfer programs, encouraging more technical preparation in high schools, increasing the use of business and industry advisory committees, increasing teaching programs sponsored by specific companies, and adapting to employees who utilize electronic communication systems and who work at home. These challenges are related to an external relations focus, primarily as it relates to feeder programs and business/industry partnerships.

Technology Challenges

The *technology challenges* cluster is comprised of four challenges: changing the curriculum in response to technological development, keeping pace with the increasing costs of technology, securing and maintaining state-of-the-art technical equipment, and increasing the use of computers in the classroom. The cluster of technology challenges is consistent with concerns expressed by administrators and faculty that all personnel should be current with technology and that technology can be used to teach more effectively and efficiently.

Program Quality Challenges

The *program quality challenges* is composed of three items: maintaining program quality, strengthening the curriculum, and maintaining a high quality faculty. Certainly this factor is consistent with those who suggest that program quality is affected by the nature of the curriculum and the quality of faculty (Chaffee & Sheer, 1992). It is also consistent with the continuous improvement philosophy (see Chaffee & Sherr, 1992; Seymour, 1993) that not only must there be appropriate inputs (faculty) and design (program elements) but also ongoing adjustments to the critical processes (strengthening and adjusting curriculum) to stay relevant and capable of meeting customers' (students, employers, etc.) needs.

External Accountability Challenges

The *external accountability challenges* cluster is comprised of three items: increasing influence and impact of state coordinating bodies; increasing influence and impact of accrediting bodies; and increasing the involvement of the U.S. government in establishing work conditions in colleges. Examination of both the popular and professional literature suggests this factor has an escalating profile, although it is clear from these data that the chairs surveyed do not anticipate having to deal with the influence of any of the three bodies to the degree that they must meet other, more pressing challenges. Many state legislatures (Mooney, 1992) as well as professional accrediting agencies are studying faculty workloads and raising challenges about the outcomes of higher education. Factors such as these raise serious accountability questions and contribute to a perception of lack of public trust in higher education institutions. Menschenfruend (1993) indicated in her review of related literature that trust has been an important issue for community colleges for more than 20 years. Still, these external factors may appear sufficiently amorphous that chairs have difficulty getting hold of them.

Curriculum Challenges

The *curriculum challenges* cluster is composed of four items: increasing general education requirements; increasing human relations training; internationalizing the curriculum; and decreasing the growth in transfer programs. All of these challenges are a part of the trend to broaden the curriculum to include learning about and experiencing different cultures and perspectives—a broader base beyond the technical knowledge and skills. The curriculum challenge is an aspect of the concern expressed by many in the business world; graduates are often inadequate or ignorant of skills and frameworks to relate to diverse audiences or, in some cases, even to a co-worker regardless of background.

Internal Accountability Challenges

The *internal accountability challenges* cluster comprises three items: using quality management techniques (e.g., TQM); addressing accountability issues; and developing efficient advisory and registration systems and procedures. The literature today is saturated with exhortations and expectations that the management of institutions is complex, requiring more effective management, leadership, and goal-setting (Likins, 1990). Developing efficient advisory and registration systems is an important challenge that appears in this grouping. Possibly this challenge suggests the importance of a "user friendly" front-end system for students, and as a high visibility mechanism to encourage attention in departments or divisions to meeting student needs.

Summary

Chairs are faced with a wide range of challenges particularly related to students, curriculum, faculty and external relations. Maintaining program quality, maintaining a high quality faculty, strengthening curriculum, and changing the curriculum in response to technological development were perceived as important by 90% or more of the chairs. The importance of these challenges has far-ranging implications for the future of community colleges.

Implications for Leadership Development

The importance of these challenges suggest attention must be paid to the following:
 • Make time, formally and informally, for discussion of the use of technology in teaching, and to develop plans for the use of technology (Albright & Graf, 1993).
 • Provide opportunities for faculty and students to have access to and practice with the new technologies.
 • Encourage faculty to visit and interact with work places that use technology. These experiences will continue to challenge faculty to stay on top of new developments and their applications.
 • Provide opportunities for faculty leadership within the institution and in the community. Delegate roles and responsibilities within established parameters and then encourage faculty to follow through in completing tasks and projects.
 • Address both long range as well as immediate faculty and staff needs in professional development programs. Provide the tools and content to enhance program quality. Provide examples of excellent staff development programs and the principles behind the programs (see Journal of Staff, Program and Organizational Development and materials developed by the NCSPOD: National Council for Staff, Program and Organizational Development, and the POD Network: Professional and Organizational Development Network.

• Provide faculty more broadening experiences to model effective human relations, and to incorporate skill and knowledge-development experiences in their classrooms.

Implications for Policy and Campus Structure

Institutional leaders must consider the following implications for institutional policy and structure:

• Develop effective and efficient processes to handle student information and interaction across the institution and within individual departments.

• Clarify the role chairs should play in working with senior faculty and in developing and encouraging effective human relationships. Green and McDade (1991) provide many suggestions.

• Assign an institutional unit responsible for maintaining the physical plant. If chairs are not given this responsibility, and few view it as crucial, someone in another administrative area must be charged with this responsibility.

• Examine institutional policies and procedures to build in work flexibility for employees.

• Encourage qualified practitioners to teach in educational programs.

• Set a priority on purchasing the technological hardware necessary to accomplish faculty and administrative goals.

• Continuously improve curricula by updating design and making adjustments in critical processes (Chaffee & Sheer, 1992; Seymour, 1993).

• Collect data from the institution's primary customers and analyze it to ensure the institution is meeting their needs (Chaffee & Sheer, 1992; Seymour, 1993).

• Carefully examine at the institutional and departmental levels, whether the advisory and registration systems are "user friendly" and present the institution's central values.

CHAPTER NINE

Strategies

What strategies do department chairs utilize in response to the challenges they face? Depending upon the chair's personality and experience, and the institutional setting, different strategies may be preferred or attempted, but a variety are utilized (Creswell et al., 1990). Whatever strategies are utilized, the chair must reflect on why they might be effective in a particular context.

To examine responses to challenges CSHPE staff developed, through applied research in community colleges and with assistance from the NCCCA, a list of potentially useful response strategies was also developed. Chairs in the survey were asked the following: **"Below are listed 24 strategies useful in addressing the challenges (identified in the prior question on the survey); indicate the extent to which you agree that the strategies would be useful to you in your current position."**

What Chairs Said

Responses to 24 strategies shown in **Table 9.1** indicated a range of agreement among chairs from a high of 92.4% to a low of 39.0%. Nearly half of the strategies were identified by 70% or more of the chairs surveyed as being useful; however, only one strategy, conducting curriculum reviews to maintain relevance (92.4%) received a 90% or more agreement level. The emphasis on curriculum is consistent with findings throughout this study of the importance of the curriculum in building and maintaining quality, and responding to community needs.

Three strategies, balancing personal and professional activities (83.7%), networking with other chairs (83.6%), and assessing future employment trends and opportunities (82.4%), received over 80% agreement. At workshops and conferences, networking with other chairs is consistently rated by participants as the greatest benefit for chair development, so this finding is not surprising. Assessing future employment trends and opportunities is necessary for program and curricular adjustments. Balancing professional and personal activities is a strategy to maintain sanity in a demanding and increasingly changing environment.

Table 9.1: Frequency Table for Strategies

Below are listed several strategies useful in addressing the challenges (identified in Chapter Eight). Indicate the extent to which you agree that the strategies would be useful to you in your current position:

Strategies	Strongly Agree (1) or Agree (2)	Neutral (3)	Disagree (4) or Strongly Disagree (5)	Mean	Std. Dev.
Conducting curriculum reviews to maintain relevance	92.4%	6.2%	1.4%	1.62	.68
Balancing personal and professional activities	83.7	12.8	3.5	1.82	.81
Networking with other chairs	83.6	13.1	3.1	1.84	.81
Assessing future employment trends and oppotunities	82.4	12.8	4.7	1.87	.86
Increasing the emphasis on long-range institutional plans	79.6	14.8	5.6	1.94	.87
Emphasizing the integration of unit plans with institutional plans	79.5	16.1	4.4	2.01	.81
Increasing staff development programs	78.0	16.8	5.2	2.02	.86
Assessing the profssional development needs of chairs	75.8	18.5	5.7	2.03	.90
Considering different approaches for allocating financial resources	74.7	20.0	5.3	2.04	.87
Building stronger partnerships with business & industry	72.0	19.4	8.7	2.07	.99
Clarifying roles and responsibilities of chairs	74.4	18.6	7.0	2.07	.93
Participating in regional conferences for chairs	67.7	23.4	9.0	2.21	.98
Developing unit mission statements	68.0	23.1	8.9	2.23	.92

Table 9.1: Frequency Table for Strategies (Cont'd)

Strategies	Strongly Agree (1) or Agree (2)	Neutral (3)	Disagree (4) or Strongly Disagree (5)	Mean	Std. Dev.
Seeking external funding	64.4	22.3	13.3	2.25	1.11
Developing campus-wide mission statements	65.0	25.5	9.5	2.26	.95
Becoming involved in mentoring	63.4	29.2	7.5	2.28	.88
Participating in a training academy for chairs	60.1	28.6	11.4	2.35	1.02
Conducting internal/external environment assessments	60.3	30.2	9.5	2.35	.93
Participating in a national conference for chairs	54.5	31.9	13.7	2.44	1.06
Providing training for clerical and service personnel	57.7	25.9	16.5	2.50	1.05
Assessing leadership styles and profiles of the chairs	50.2	35.3	14.4	2.53	1.00
Writing job descriptions for chairs	50.6	33.7	15.8	2.55	1.03
Participating in formal graduate courses	46.8	32.5	20.8	2.66	1.10
Reviewing and revising the organizational chart	39.0	39.8	21.2	2.79	1.03

Ranked in order of importance by mean score
Legend: Strongly Agree = 1; Agree = 2; Neutral = 3; Disagree = 4; Strongly Disagree = 5.

Seven strategies were perceived as important by 70% or more of the chairs: increasing the emphasis on long-range institutional planning (79.6%), emphasizing the integration of unit plans with institutional plans (79.5%), increasing staff development programs (78.0%), assessing professional development needs of chairs (75.8%), considering different approaches for allocating financial resources (74.7%), clarifying roles and responsibilities of chairs (74.4%), and building stronger partnerships with business and industry (72.0%). Several of these strategies address planning, both long-range and short-range, which is a clear expectation in most units. This planning perspective is consistent with the strong support for the planning task detailed in Chapter Six. Two strategies, one for staff and the other for chairs, indicates the importance of continuous professional development—a necessity for any organization to remain current and productive.

Seven strategies were rated as important by 60% or more of the chairs, indicating considerable variation in response. These included: developing unit mission statements (68.0%), participating in regional conferences for chairs (67.7%), developing campus-wide mission statements (65.0%), seeking external funding (64.4%), becoming involved in mentoring (63.4%), conducting internal/external environment assessments (60.3%), and participating in a training academy for chairs (60.1%). Again, planning and continued chair development are the primary strategies identified at this level. Planning strategies are oriented both internally (unit mission statements and campus-wide mission statements) and externally (internal/external assessments and seek external funding). Once again, consistent with findings in Chapter Six: Roles, mentoring as a tool for working with faculty was not highly valued.

Four strategies, providing training for clerical and service personnel (57.7%), participating in a national conference for chairs (54.5%), writing job descriptions for chairs (50.6%), and assessing leadership styles and profiles of the chairs (50.2%), were perceived by 50% or more of the chairs as important. All four have standard deviations of 1.0 or greater, indicating considerable variability in agreement. Three of these strategies are related to chair definition (write chairs' job description) and development (leadership style and participation in a national chair academy). The fourth strategy addresses clerical training. These strategies may not have been rated as important because many chairs already have job descriptions, believe they have established their leadership style, and presume they provide enough clerical training. They also may not know enough about the newly established, unique National Community College Chair Academy at Maricopa Community College (Mesa, Arizona) to see its relevance for them, may already participate, or they see it as beyond their means. On a less optimistic note, it is possible these chairs simply do not understand the importance of these strategies in their work, despite the calls in the literature for greater chair preparation (Hammons & Wallace, 1977).

Two strategies, participating in formal graduate courses (46.8%) and reviewing and revising the organizational chart (39.0%) were the least favored. Both had standard deviations of over 1.0 and over half of the respondents were neutral or disagreed with their importance. This response suggests that many chairs do not perceive formal graduate courses, possibly because of their theoretical nature, as relevant to improving their effectiveness as chairs or believe conferences and workshops to be sufficient. The low rating for revising the organizational chart may indicate the lack of relevance to the chair, the existence of a decentralized system with considerable autonomy, or the appropriateness of their current chart. Even 10 years ago, developing organizational charts as an important response strategy would probably have been rated higher.

Strategies Clusters

When a factor analysis was performed to combine items and identify similarities among strategy responses, the 24 strategies reduced to four clusters as shown in **Table 9.2**.

Table 9.2. Strategies Clusters

Chair Development Strategies
- Assessing leadership styles and profiles of chairs
- Writing job descriptions for chairs
- Participating in a training academy for chairs
- Participating in regional conferences for chairs
- Participating in a national conference for chairs
- Participating in formal graduate courses
- Reviewing and revising the organizational chart
- Providing training for clerical and service personnel
- Clarifying roles and responsibilities of chairs
- Assessing the professional development needs of chairs
- Networking with other chairs

Planning Strategies
- Increasing the emphasis on long-range institutional planning
- Developing unit mission statements
- Developing campus-wide mission statements
- Conducting internal/external assessments
- Emphasizing the integration of unit plans with institutional plans
- Conducting curriculum reviews to maintain relevance

Table 9.2. Strategies Clusters (Cont'd)

Personal & Professional Development Strategies
- Increasing staff development programs
- Becoming involved in mentoring
- Balancing personal & professional activities

External and Financial Strategies
- Assessing future employment trends and opportunities
- Considering different approaches for allocating financial resources
- Seeking external funding
- Building stronger partnerships with business and industry

Chair Development Strategies

The *chair development strategies* cluster is composed of 11 strategies: assessing chairs' leadership styles and profiles, writing chairs' job descriptions, participating in a training academy, participating in regional conferences, participating in a national conference, participating in formal graduate courses, reviewing and revising the organizational chart, providing clerical and service personnel training, clarifying chairs' roles and responsibilities, assessing chairs' professional development needs, and networking with other chairs. The cluster emphasizes assessment, training, job descriptions, and networking. It reinforces the importance of a clear job description as identified in a prior study (Winner, 1989). With the exception of providing clerical and service personnel training, all of the strategies address activities that directly encourage chair development (assessing, networking, coursework, workshops, and job descriptions). However, providing clerical and service personnel training is related, because what the chair can address is partly determined by the confidence that office operations are in competent hands.

Planning Strategies

The *planning strategies* cluster demonstrates that chairs who agree with the importance of planning do so in all areas. Six institutional strategies clustered together: conducting internal/external environmental assessments, developing unit mission statements, increasing the emphasis on long-range institutional planning, emphasizing the integration of unit plans with institutional plans, conducting curricular reviews to maintain relevance, and developing campus-wide mission statements. These strategies demonstrate a strong commitment to the long-term health of the department and the institution, and are consistent with an institutional focus—a strong emphasis on planning. This cluster suggests that department or division effectiveness depends upon systematic use of comprehensive planning.

Personal and Professional Development Cluster

The *personal and professional development strategies* cluster is composed of three strategies: increasing staff development programs, becoming involved in mentoring, and balancing personal and professional activities. This cluster is focused upon others: being personally committed to encouraging faculty and staff to continue to grow and develop professionally, while finding a balance with personal interests and responsibilities. Much of the chair literature, particularly Tucker (1984), Creswell et al. (1990), and Boice (1992), indicate the importance of the chair facilitating the growth and development of others. Support for this is also found in the literature about community college chairs or division heads (Scott, 1990; Lamb, 1993). Chair knowledge of the institutional resource system and other opportunities available to meet the needs of faculty and staff will result in greater success.

External and Financial Strategies

The *external and financial strategies* cluster is composed of four strategies, three of which are primarily externally focused. The strategies include: assessing future employment trends and opportunities, seeking external funding, building stronger partnerships with business and industry, and considering different approaches for allocating financial resources. The literature on continuous improvement (e.g., Chaffee & Scheer, 1992; Seymour, 1993) indicates that clarifying customer needs, building partnerships, and providing appropriate training are all relevant to any unit's development. Different approaches for allocating resources may cluster with other items noted because of its relationship to external factors.

Summary

Chairs use a wide range of strategies to meet the challenges and needs of their situations. The most important of these are assessing future employment trends and opportunities and conducting curriculum reviews for relevance, and on a more personal level, networking with other chairs and finding a balance for professional activities. The strategies breakout into four clusters as the means to carry out goals and plans of a department: chair development, planning, personal and professional development (for others), and external and financial strategies. To move the institution forward, chairs and institutions need to select those strategies that are appropriate to their environment and consider the following implications.

Implications for Leadership Development

Community college chairs can apply the strategies identified in the chapter for their own development by attending to the following suggestions:
• Participate in and develop chair networking within and outside the college.
• Model a balance between professional and personal life, and encourage faculty and staff to do the same.
• Develop systematic professional development programs to encourage staff to gain necessary skills and knowledge (Schuster & Wheeler, 1990).
• Understand that chairs will be required to mentor as well as evaluate staff (Sorcinelli & Austin, 1992; Wunsch, in press) and must support other chairs in the mentor role.
• Develop skills in relating externally and developing coalitions.
• Use a range of activities to meet chairs' professional development needs (Green & McDade, 1991; McDade, 1987). Emphasize the need to balance immediate, short-term development with long-term development which incorporates theory, practice, and reflection.

Implications for Policy and Campus Structure

Institutions can support chairs in their application of identified crucial strategies in several key ways:
• Expect chairs to clarify role expectations and responsibilities with faculty and upper administrators (Seagren, Creswell, & Wheeler, 1993).
• Develop and expect a norm of continuous professional development at the institutional level and develop a systematic program of development (Schuster & Wheeler, 1990).
• Encourage chairs to be knowledgeable about and utilize all available resources for staff development (Green & McDade, 1991).
• Expect chairs to continually search for outside funding, and then be good stewards of those funds in internal appropriations.

• Design comprehensive, integrated administrative systems which provide chairs the information and mechanisms needed to effectively manage financial resources.

• Develop a systematic plan to aid chair development (Seagren, Creswell, & Wheeler, 1993; Tucker, 1992).

• Provide opportunities for chairs to perfect planning skills (Cope, 1987).

CHAPTER TEN

Influences of Selected Characteristics on Chair Responses

Part I of this book included a discussion of 45 demographic items from responses to the Community College Chair survey, and revealed information about chairs, their units, and their institutions. Prior chapters in Part II described chair perceptions of job dimensions. Such information aids understanding of chair beliefs, values, roles, tasks, and skills, the challenges chairs face, and the strategies employed in response to those challenges.

Researchers often investigate how demographic characteristics influence responses to other survey questions. The range in responses to several job dimensions logically led to questions as to whether certain chair characteristics, or types of units or campuses, might account for variation in the survey responses received. For example, are chairs who have a background in business or industry likely to view financial accountability issues as significant to their roles? Are chairs who are responsible for greater numbers of faculty concerned with interpersonal issues or professional development?

This chapter describes relationships in the data, and answers the broad question: **What differences exist between chairs, their units and their institutions in their perceptions of job dimensions?**

The community college chair data base contained 143 job dimensions in addition to the 45 demographics noted above. Given the magnitude of the data base, individual comparisons were determined to be unrealistic. However, the item clustering process described in Chapter One resulted in 28 clusters, which have been identified and described throughout Chapters Four through Nine, and allowed researchers to identify differences in a manageable way. Sixteen of the survey's 45 demographic items, shown in **Table 10.1**, were selected for the analysis based on a review of the literature and an examination of items from the survey which showed wide variation.

Table 10.1. Characteristics Selected for Analysis

Chair Characteristics
- age
- gender
- race
- years as chair
- experience in education
  (collapsed from three items: K-12, 4-year colleges, and university
  or professional school)
- public agency experience
- business and industry experience
- vocational or technical school experience
- appointment limited to a specific term
- professional plans for the next five years

Unit Characteristics
- present position (Head, Chair, Other)
- student headcount in unit
  (collapsed to <400, 400-800, >800)
- number of full-time faculty in unit
  (collapsed to <10, 10-20, >20)
- number of part-time faculty in unit
  (collapsed to <10, 10-20, >20)
- primary program area
  (utilized four largest areas: liberal arts & sciences, general studies,
  nursing & allied health, and business administration & accounting)

Campus Characteristics
- instructional focus of the campus

Each of the 16 demographic characteristics affected responses in at least one cluster. Seven accounted for variation in half or more of the clusters, and are the focus of this chapter. A matrix showing the full results of these seven comparisons is included as **Table 10.2**. The following sections explore in detail how these characteristics impacted responses.

Table 10.2: Characteristics with Job Dimensions

	Q.5 Part-Time Faculty	Q.8 Program Area	Q.22 Gender	Q.23 Race	Q.27 Business/ Industry Experience	Q.32 Vocational/ Technical Experience	Q.33 Appt. Limited
BELIEF 1: Beliefs About Curriculum and Students	.0420	.1543	.0000*	.0000*	.5060	.0054*	.0113
BELIEF 2: Beliefs About Mission and Access	.0000*	.0000*	.0000*	.9519	.0000*	.0000*	.0998
ROLE 1: Interpersonal Role	.0000*	.1930	.0000*	.1288	.0684	.0030*	.5024
ROLE 2: Administrator Role	.0000*	.0247	.0002*	.0266	.2890	.0278	.0047*
ROLE 3: Leader Role	.0147	.0000*	.0000*	.0017*	.0000*	.0000*	.0000*
TASK 1: Professional Development and Communication Tasks	.0000*	.0509	.0000*	.0000*	.4449	.0009*	.0004*
TASK 2: Faculty Selection and Feedback Tasks	.0008*	.3652	.0009*	.0152	.6524	.0151	.0000*
TASK 3: Budget Tasks	.0010*	.1289	.0119	.6906	.5827	.0369	.0007*
TASK 4: Internal Tasks	.0213	.0001*	.1130	.0002*	.0096*	.0003*	.0000*
TASK 5: External Tasks	.0000*	.0000*	.0026*	.0007*	.0000*	.0000*	.0000*
TASK 6: Curriculum and Student Tasks	.0000*	.0010*	.0036*	.0031*	.0039*	.6307	.0437

*Cells significant at ≤ .01 alpha

Table 10.2: Characteristics with Job Dimensions (Cont'd)

	Q.5 Part-Time Faculty	Q.8 Program Area	Q.22 Gender	Q.23 Race	Q.27 Business/ Industry Experience	Q.32 Vocational/ Technical Experience	Q.33 Appt. Limited
TASK 7: Planning Tasks	.0951	.0000*	.0000*	.0000*	.0742	.0050*	.0633
SKILL 1: Administrative Skills and Leadership	.0025*	.0001*	.0000*	.1613	.0013*	.0001*	.0159
SKILL 2: Interpersonal Skills	.1672	.1214	.0000*	.0066*	.0521	.0926	.1977
SKILL 3: Individual Skills	.0543	.1525	.0000*	.0038*	.0002*	.0003*	.0000*
CHALLENGE 1: Faculty Challenges	.0024*	.7276	.0000*	.0000*	.1269	.0010*	.0114
CHALLENGE 2: Student Challenges	.0006*	.0401	.0000*	.0000*	.8914	.5026	.0000*
CHALLENGE 3: External Relations Challenges	.0049*	.0000*	.0508	.0000*	.0000*	.0000*	.0000*
CHALLENGE 4 Technology Challenges	.5435	.0000*	.0004*	.0277	.0000*	.0000*	.0007*
CHALLENGE 5: Program Quality Challenges	.4924	.0007*	.0001*	.0928	.0028*	.0016*	.0123

*Cells significant at ≤ .01 alpha

Table 10.2: Characteristics with Job Dimensions (Cont'd)

	Q.5 Part-Time Faculty	Q.8 Program Area	Q.22 Gender	Q.23 Race	Q.27 Business/ Industry Experience	Q.32 Vocational/ Technical Experience	Q.33 Appt. Limited
CHALLENGE 6: External Accountability Challenges	.1189	.0374	.0016*	.0164	.0294	.0095*	.0246
CHALLENGE 7: Financial Resources Challenges	.8604	.0007*	.1593	.2786	.0185	.5491	.9590
CHALLENGE 8: Curriculum Challenges	.0027*	.0000*	.0013*	.0000*	.5918	.7467	.0002*
CHALLENGE 9: Internal Accountability Challenges	.8141	.0000*	.0000*	.0001*	.0000*	.0000*	.0000*
STRATEGY 1: Chair Development Strategies	.0003*	.0768	.0000*	.0000*	.1279	.0001*	.0000*
STRATEGY 2: Planning Strategies	.3597	.0310	.0000*	.0000*	.0002*	.0000*	.0001*
STRATEGY 3: Personal and Developmental Strategies	.0138	.1048	.0000*	.0000*	.0049*	.0000*	.0071*
STRATEGY 4: External and Financial Strategies	.5006	.0000*	.0001*	.0057*	.0000*	.0000*	.0000*

*Cells significant at ≤ .01 alpha

Chair Characteristics

Gender

The research question which guided this analysis was: **Is there a difference between male and female responses to job dimensions?** A considerable body of research has emerged in recent years suggesting that women exhibit differing personal and leadership/management styles than men (Gilligan, 1983; Helgesen, 1990; Belenky et al., 1991). Thus, gender was selected as one of the important characteristics to examine for its influence on responses.

Gender influenced responses in more clusters than any other of the selected demographic items; differences were present in 24 of the 28 clusters. Across all factors, women were more likely than men to agree with beliefs, strategies and challenges, and to find skills, roles and tasks as important.

Female chairs agreed with the statements clustered under *Beliefs about Curriculum and Students* more often than did male chairs, with a similar but less pronounced difference for statements clustered under *Beliefs about Mission and Access*. Women were more likely than men to view as important items in the three role clusters *Interpersonal Role, Administrator Role,* and *Leader Role* than men.

With respect to the importance of items in the task and skill clusters, differences between male and female respondents were found in 8 of 10 clusters. Female chairs were more likely than male chairs to identify as important items clustered under *Professional Development and Communication Tasks, Curriculum and Student Tasks, Faculty Selection and Feedback Tasks,* and *Administrative Skills and Leadership.*

Responses in the cluster *Interpersonal Skills* showed less variation than the others, however the pattern of female chairs viewing items as more important persisted. Many of the items in these clusters show a responsibility to other individuals. They are supported by broader theories of a female propensity toward an ethic of care for others (Gilligan, 1983), information processing through interaction (Belenky et al., 1991), and other-centered leadership (Helgesen, 1990).

Female chairs were also more likely to believe in the importance of items in two other task clusters: *External Tasks* and *Planning Tasks,* as well as in the skills cluster *Individual Skills.*

Seven of the nine clusters in the challenges section showed response differences due to gender. Women's item responses were distributed relatively evenly across the scale in the *Faculty Challenges* cluster, while men's responses tended toward the disagreement end of the scale. In the six clusters *Student Challenges, Technology*

Challenges, Program Quality Challenges, External Accountability Challenges, Curriculum Challenges, and *Internal Accountability Challenges,* female chairs selected responses on the agree to neutral end of the scale while male chairs more consistently selected responses in the neutral to disagree range.

All four clusters of strategies showed response differences by gender. Female chairs were much more likely than male counterparts to agree with items included in the *Chair Development Strategies, Planning Strategies, Personal and Development Strategies,* and *External and Financial Strategies* clusters.

Overall, male and female chairs appear to view their own preferred job dimensions, challenges and strategies differently. Men made greater distinctions in their responses than the women, who tended to rate most items with a greater degree of importance. Such a gender bias is often found in research which makes use of Likert-type rating scales (Spitzack, 1988). Nevertheless, this finding suggests that the implementation of strategies for continued growth and development should be influenced by and inclusive of gender-related frameworks.

Race

Although few racial minorities were identified in the chair data base, an important question was whether race accounted for some of the differences apparent in survey responses. The research question addressed was **Does race account for any differences in chair perspectives on job dimensions?** Although minimal literature exists on management styles of cultural groups (see Kimmons, 1977; Morrison, 1992) the size of this data base made a comparison worth reviewing.

All ethnic respondents were collapsed into a single category to compare against Caucasian chairs; following this process, chairs' race showed significant differences within 18 of the 28 clusters, demonstrating race as impacting responses in the third largest number of clusters. Responses followed a pattern similar to that of the gender differentiation: ethnic chairs generally responded more favorably in the clusters than did Caucasian chairs.

Consistent with this pattern, ethnic chairs more often agreed with items in the cluster *Beliefs About Curriculum and Students* than their Caucasian counterparts. This cluster included items related to the enrollment of minority students, offering courses for students of limited English-speaking ability, and serving at-risk students. The cluster *Beliefs About Mission and Access* did not show response differences by race. These results show that while most community college chairs are committed to their inherent mission of access, racial differences exist with respect to specifics of how access might be guaranteed.

Ethnic chairs ascribed more importance than Caucasian chairs to items in several role, task and skills clusters: *Leader Role, Professional Development and Communication Tasks, Internal Tasks, External Tasks, Curriculum and Student Tasks, Planning Tasks, Interpersonal Skills,* and *Individual Skills.*

For nine of the 13 challenges and strategies clusters, response differences by race were found. Ethnic chairs more frequently agreed with items included in the clusters *Faculty Challenges, Student Challenges, External Relations Challenges, Curriculum Challenges, Internal Accountability Challenges, Chair Development Strategies, Personal and Development Strategies,* and *Planning Strategies,* while Caucasian chairs more frequently were neutral or disagreed.

It is clear the ethnic respondents have strong commitments to their relationships with students and faculty, as well as the external constituents who can impact their programs. Yet, they also agree with the importance of diverse administrative tasks. They have a broad view of the community college mission and its diverse purposes, and attempt to balance a range of priorities. Like the female chairs outlined previously, ethnic chairs do not distinguish between job dimensions to the extent that Caucasian chairs do, and therefore may find the position particularly challenging.

Prior Experience in a Vocational/Technical College

Although only 17.5% of the respondents had prior administrative experience in a vocational/technical setting, a research question was framed around this issue: **Does prior experience in a Vocational/Technical College or Institute influence respondent perspectives of job dimensions?** It seemed important to examine how experience directly related to the current role would influence responses. To the extent that community colleges have a culture and norms of their own (Birnbaum, 1988), it follows that chairs who have been immersed in that culture might view their positions from a different perspective than those not socialized in that culture.

When analyzed, this item impacted responses in 20 of the 28 clusters, the second most frequent comparison. In general terms, chairs with prior experience in a vocational setting were more likely to select agree or important responses, while chairs without prior experience in the setting responded with disagree or not important responses.

Chairs with prior experience in a vocational or technical setting were more likely to view as important items in the clusters *Interpersonal Role, Internal Tasks,* and *Administrative Skills and Leadership.* They also more often agreed with items included in the *Faculty Challenges, Program Quality Challenges* and *Internal Accountability Challenges* clusters. These clusters include items which demonstrate a commitment to taking care of business in-house first, and may reflect a sensitivity to their administrative role (Ferguson, 1993).

Chairs with prior experience more often agreed with items in the *Beliefs About Curriculum and Students* and *Beliefs About Mission and Access* clusters than chairs without prior experience. They also agreed to a greater extent with items included in the clusters *External Relations Challenges, Technology Challenges* and *External Accountability Challenges*, as well as to all four strategy clusters. On job dimensions measured by the importance scale, experienced chairs more often responded with important to items included in the clusters *Leader Role, Professional Development and Communication Tasks, External Tasks, Planning Tasks* and *Individual Skills*.

As noted earlier, the diverse group against which chairs with prior vocational/ technical experience were compared comprised all other respondents, including those with other types of educational experience. Still, it is fair to conclude that chairs with particular vocational or technical experience seem well socialized to the culture of the community college and are more cognizant of the foundation of beliefs and values which are in place to guide their practice. Conversely, it may be that experience within other settings broadens chairs' perspectives about the importance of a variety of their job dimensions, and the necessity of their leadership with respect to a myriad matters. Such a broad view may allow chairs without directly related prior experience to make greater distinctions between the most important aspects of their positions.

Prior Experience in Business and Industry

A research question was developed to explore the question: **Is there a difference in respondent perspectives on job dimensions based on whether or not they have had prior work experience in business or industry?** Relationships between prior experience in business and industry and how a chair might view the chair role are steeped in the same assumptions made about individuals with prior experience in vocational or technical schools. Exposure shapes attitudes and behavior.

Within this category, chairs either had prior experience or did not; the question gave no indication as to the length of time in the experience or situation. Chairs who had previously worked in business and industry agreed with or responded with important in greater numbers than their peers without such experience to items included in all 14 of the 28 clusters impacted. Chairs with prior business or industry experience more often agreed with items included in the clusters *Beliefs About Mission and Access, External Relations Challenges, Technology Challenges, Program Quality Challenges, Internal Accountability Challenges, Planning*

Strategies, Personal and Development Strategies, and *External and Financial Strategies*. Chairs without such experience were more likely to disagree with items in these clusters. Within the role, task and skill clusters, chairs with business exposure ranked with greater importance items in six clusters: *Leader Role, Internal Tasks, External Tasks, Curriculum and Student Tasks, Administrative Skills and Leadership*, and *Individual Skills*.

These results indicate that chairs with more traditional business backgrounds see the need for processes and strategies around planning, leadership, faculty development and external responsiveness. Such foci may result in programs with greater external and curricular relevance.

Appointment Limited to a Specific Term

To assess whether the term of a chair's appointment might impact responses, the research question was framed: **Is there a difference in item responses between those chairs who have a limited term appointment, and those who do not?** Particular job dimensions may be given greater weight dependent upon a chair's perspective toward the short- or long-term. One-third of survey respondents had a limited appointment, although most of those appointments were renewable.

Differences in responses based on whether or not a chair was serving a limited term occurred in 17 of the 28 clusters. Chairs with unlimited appointments generally agreed with or viewed as important more of the survey items in the clusters.

Chairs with unlimited terms thought items included in the clusters *Administrator Role* and *Professional Development and Communication Tasks* were much more important than their peers with limited terms. To a lesser degree, they also ascribed more importance to items included in the *Leader Role, Faculty Selection and Feedback Tasks, Budget Tasks, Internal Tasks, External Tasks*, and *Individual Skills* clusters.

The unlimited term chairs more often agreed with challenges facing them clustered under *Student Challenges, External Relations Challenges, Technology Challenges, Curriculum Challenges*, and *Internal Accountability Challenges* than chairs with limited terms. A similar dynamic was found with respect to the usefulness of items in all four strategies clusters.

These results point to a presumption that chairs who are in their positions for the long term hold a broader view of their responsibilities, and have a greater commitment to long-term results. The findings also support the notion that short-term chairs have the freedom to focus less on administrative issues (Smith, 1992). With respect to their faculty, it makes sense that short-term chairs view themselves less as leaders and more as facilitators among peers; as such they will be less likely to take responsibility for faculty selection and development or internal relations issues. It is likewise understandable that limited term chairs would be likely to focus less energy on developing external relations. It is somewhat surprising that limited term chairs were less interested in exploiting opportunities for their own growth and development while in that role; perhaps they view the appointment as secondary to maintaining teaching expertise in their discipline.

Unit Characteristics

Part-Time Faculty

An analysis was completed to answer the question **Does the number of part-time faculty in a unit influence chair perceptions of job dimensions?** Certainly the size of a unit will influence the variety and job functions performed by a chair, and so will the number and type of faculty with whom the chair must interact because of issues of greater decentralization, delegation, and the like (Seagren, Creswell, & Wheeler, 1993).

For 14 of the 28 clusters, the number of part-time faculty in the unit significantly impacted how respondents answered questions. As one might suspect, the greatest differentiation came between institutions of either less than 10 or more than 20 part-time faculty, with the 11-20 range responding more frequently to the norm. This suggests that very small and very large departments not only operate differently from one another, but also from what might be "typical."

Chairs in units with fewer part-time faculty more often agreed with, or found as important, items in the clusters *Beliefs About Mission and Access, External Tasks,* and *External Relations Challenges.* They provided opposite responses to chairs from campuses with more than 20 faculty on the *Planning Tasks* cluster, responding more frequently with important than chairs with a greater number of part-time faculty, who responded to items in this cluster more often in the neutral to not important range. This particular finding is counterintuitive, as one might expect a larger staff to require greater planning. Perhaps some latitude in maintaining a larger staff of part-time faculty allows chairs to be less concerned about long-range planning, or in involving part-time faculty in unit meetings, campus committees, and the like. Further, part-time faculty may be viewed as less central to decision-making.

In several other clusters, the chairs with fewer unit part-time faculty more frequently disagreed with items or viewed them as less important than their peers with larger numbers of staff. This disparity occurred in the challenge and strategies clusters *Faculty Challenges, Student Challenges, Curriculum Challenges*, and *Chair Development Strategies.* Less importance was also ascribed by chairs with fewer part-time faculty to items in role, task and skill clusters *Interpersonal Role, Administrator Role, Professional Development and Communication Tasks, Faculty Selection and Feedback Tasks, Budget Tasks*, and *Administrative Skills and Leadership.* These chairs appear less concerned about relationships with selection and development of their faculty, than chairs with greater numbers of part-time staff. This may be a function of unit or institutional size in general, as well as a function of unit resources, if increasing funding follows increasing size.

In total, 10 of the 14 significant clusters generally reflect greater agreement or importance ascribed to items by chairs with larger part-time teaching staffs. If the assumption that units with greater numbers of part-time faculty are also larger units is accurate, these findings would support the notion that chairs of larger departments feel pulled by varied priorities, most or all of which seem important (Gmelch & Miskin, 1993). Making distinctions between priorities may be a more difficult task for these chairs.

Primary Program Area

One hypothesis centered around the possibility that differences might be found in how chairs from different program areas respond to survey items. The question **Does academic program area influence respondent perspectives on job dimensions?** was framed to address this assumption. This analysis was completed using the four program areas with the greatest number of survey responses: Liberal Arts & Sciences, Nursing & Allied Health, Business Administration & Accounting, and General Studies.

When chair responses across the four program areas were compared against one another, differences were found in 14 of the 28 clusters. In all instances, the greatest difference in responses could be attributed to either the liberal arts or the nursing and allied health chairs. In three of the cases, business administration and accounting chairs also contributed to the variation.

Pronounced differences were found in chairs of departments of liberal arts and sciences, who were more likely to disagree with or view as unimportant items in nine clusters: *Beliefs About Mission and Access, Leader Role, External Tasks, Planning Tasks, External Relations Challenges, Technology Challenges, Financial Resources Challenges*, and *Internal Accountability Challenges.* Since the belief cluster included items related to occupational & technical education, preparing students for business and industry, and establishing external committees to establish the curriculum, response differences were logical and predictable. These are the departments within community colleges who see themselves least likely to benefit from or answer to external constituents; practical applications and skill development are not typically viewed as significant to liberal arts programs, many of which exist for academic transfer. Funding and accountability issues were also not seen by liberal arts and sciences chairs as being as important as was true for chairs in nursing and allied health and/or business administration and accounting. Finally, the liberal arts chairs were less likely than any other group to agree with the importance of items in the task cluster *Curriculum and Student Tasks*, perhaps because the liberal arts curriculum is less reactive to occupational needs.

Six of the distinctions noted above are similar to some reported earlier: *Beliefs About Mission and Access, Leader Role, Individual Skills, External Tasks, External Relations Challenges, Technology Challenges, Internal Accountability Challenges* and *External and Financial Strategies*. Responses provided by the liberal arts chairs virtually replicate those given by chairs without business or industry experience. These educational traditionalists view the community college similar to chairs who have not been exposed to organizations outside of education, and clearly have a more focused view of their roles.

Nursing and allied health chairs believed in greater numbers than other program chairs in the importance of items included in the clusters *Internal Tasks* and *Administrative Skills and Leadership*. These programs have been growing in importance in recent years (Adelman, 1992), as such, attention within the department may be a priority. Opposing responses were most often given by business administration and accounting chairs on *Internal Task* items; by liberal arts chairs on *Administrative Skills and Leadership* items. The nursing and allied health chairs disagreed more often than any other group with items related to *Curriculum Challenges*; again this may be due to significant changes which have already been made and accreditation guidelines which are already in place. Across all groups there were neutral to disagree responses for items included in the *Program Quality Challenges* cluster. Within this narrow range, however, nursing and allied health chairs were more often neutral in their responses, while liberal arts chairs were in greater disagreement with items.

Summary

Although the community college database provides a picture of the typical chair, with his or her job dimensions prioritized, it is clear from the more indepth relational analyses that wide discrepancies exist in how chairs view their jobs. It is also apparent that most chairs take their roles quite seriously, attempting to meet widely ranging expectations, particularly given the limited concrete rewards which accompany the position.

Seven demographic characteristics accounted for variation in responses to items included in half or more of the 28 clusters generated from this study. "Gender" most frequently influenced how individuals responded to the survey questions; variations existed between the responses of men and women for 24 of the 28 clusters. Of next highest importance was the characteristic "Prior Experience in a Vocational/Technical College or Institute"; 20 of the 28 clusters showed differences in responses based on whether the respondent had previously worked in a vocational or technical setting. The characteristic which impacted the next greatest number of clusters was "Race"; ethnic and Caucasian respondents answered questions differently in 18 clusters. Closely behind race was the characteristic "Appointment as Chair/ Head Limited to a Specific Term," which demonstrated response differences for 17 of the 28 clusters. Three other characteristics showed statistically significant variations for 14 of the 28 clusters; those were "Number of Part-time Faculty," "Program Area," and "Prior Experience in Business and Industry."

The distinctions noted here provide background from which to assess and address personal styles and biases that can enhance and hinder chair effectiveness. These comparisons can be utilized for self-knowledge, as a model for personal and professional development, or as a framework for chair development. More than anything else, the survey findings demonstrate that all chairs do not think in similar fashion nor speak with one voice, particularly within the heterogeneous community college culture.

Implications for Leadership Development

Chairs must have the capacity to build on the strengths of their institutions and resources, appreciate the widely differing backgrounds that other chairs bring to their positions and learn from one another, develop clear priorities for what is reasonable to accomplish, and be conscious about their own development for improved effectiveness in the administrative role they have accepted. Many chairs must also pay closer attention to relationships within and outside of the department, moving from strict task management to human resource management and development as well. Specific recommendations include:

• Learn from other chairs through internal and external networking around interests and needs (Green & McDade, 1991).

• Female and ethnic chairs need to set priorities about their work as chairs. Their agendas may be too ambitious, with a desire to make everything a high priority. One explanation may be that these chairs are trying to "make it" in an environment still predominated by white males. However, burn-out serves no one's ends. Participation in a range of activities such as simulations and case studies might assist these chairs in reflecting on their approaches to see if changes are needed. Conversely, majority male chairs may need to self-check to determine whether they are becoming complacent or too narrow in their focus.

• If chairs have not had experience outside academe, they should be encouraged to learn more about how work and the learning environment interface and complement one another.

Implications for Policy and Campus Structure

• If the institution wants to have more integration and involvement with business and community, it may want to select more chairs with experience beyond academe.

• Different needs in departments can be better met by using the findings on chair personal characteristics. For example, more female and ethnic chairs show greater commitment to a range of chair behaviors that are important to institutional and individual development and should be encouraged to exploit those abilities. Other chairs may need to take advantage of development opportunities in these areas as well.

• Institutions should clarify their expectations for long-term, continuous leadership and select chairs who meet the criteria.

PART III:

SUMMARY AND REFLECTIONS

CHAPTER ELEVEN

Profile, Discussion and Future Research

The community college appears to have an increasingly important role to play in postsecondary education; its programs have increased dramatically in size, scope and complexity in the past two and a half decades. Due to these developments and changes, the chair/head of the department/division has an increasingly important role, and the number and complexity of responsibilities has increased. Although department chairs in four-year institutions have been extensively studied, few efforts have focused solely on the community college chair. In addition, most of the leadership development programs available for community college personnel have focused on positions other than the chair. Therefore, there was a need for emphasizing leadership development for chairs/heads in community colleges. The National Community College Chair Academy (NCCCA) was created to respond to this need for leadership development for chair training.

Early in 1992, NCCCA contracted with the Center for the Study of Higher and Postsecondary Education (CSHPS) at the University of Nebraska-Lincoln to conduct a survey of community college chairs to develop a profile of chairs, departments and campuses of community colleges; to identify areas or topics perceived to be important for inclusion in academic leadership development programs; to identify policy and structural implications; and, to identify research topics which need to be studied. CSHPS staff developed a conceptual model of the departmental chair to guide this effort. The model provided the basis for development of the survey, which included nine dimensions: demographic information, characteristics of the instructional unit, characteristics of the campus, beliefs and values, roles, tasks, skills, challenges, and strategies. The survey was mailed to approximately 9,000 academic leaders in U.S. and Canadian community colleges by NCCCA. A total of 2,875 usable returns were received, yielding a response rate of 32%. The following profile provides a "snapshot" from the survey results related to the characteristics of chairs, departments, campuses and job dimensions, a discussion of the implications for leadership development and institutions and, finally, a section dealing with issues needing further study.

Profile

What could one "typically" expect to find when walking into the office of a "chair" in a "department" on a community college "campus"? From the responses to the survey, in the early part of the decade of the '90s, we have some answers.

The Chair

The individual occupying the position which provides leadership to the academic unit in the community college is likely to:
- have a name plate which lists the title of "chair";
- be a 45-54 year old Caucasian, who has earned a Master's degree;
- have community college experience of 6-10 years in the chair role, 11-15 years in a faculty role, but none in other administrative roles;
- have prior experience working in business/industry; and,
- have previous experience in some other educational setting (either K-12 schools, a university or professional school, a four-year college, or a vocational/technical school) or a public agency.

The chair is most likely to have an appointment that:
- is made by an administrator rather than faculty election;
- is renewable;
- provides release time from teaching of 3 classes;
- has an annual salary between $41,000-60,000;
- includes a chair stipend of $1,501-2,000; and,
- requires 31-40 hours per week in leadership/management functions beyond the time required for teaching.

The typical chair appears to be in a stable career position. Over the next five years the individual in this position plans to:
- stay at the same community college; and,
- remain in the chair role.

The Department

The survey provided information about the characteristics of the work environment, in addition to the position itself. The unit is likely to:
- be identified as a "department";
- have been in operation 16-20 years;
- enroll 401-600 full-time and part-time students (headcount);
- employ 11-20 full-time and another 11-20 part-time faculty;

116

- offer an Associate of Arts or Associate of Applied Science degree program if located in the United States, or Diploma program in Canada; and,
- have the largest enrollments in the Liberal Arts and Sciences, Nursing and Allied Health, or Business Administration and Accounting programs.

The Campus

The survey also provided information about the characteristics of the campus in which this chair and department function. The "average" community college campus:

- enrolls 4,001-6,000 full-time and another 4,001-6,000 part-time students;
- employs 101-150 full-time and another 101-150 part-time faculty members;
- has 11-20 persons functioning in chair roles, who are appointed by the administration;
- is comprehensive, offering both technical and transfer programs; and,
- is publicly funded, with primary support coming from the state or province.

Job Dimensions

The chair is guided by a set of **beliefs and values**, ideally consistent with the mission of the community college. Based on the responses to the survey, the chair is committed to:

- the concept of life-long learning;
- general as well as occupational/technical education;
- preparing students to meet the needs of the community as much as the needs of business and industry;
- encouraging faculty to use a wide variety of teaching approaches, and using computers in the classroom;
- providing students in-depth knowledge through a major;
- providing learning skills through developmental courses;
- promoting and encouraging the enrollment of minority students;
- offering students support services; and,
- providing opportunities for students to experience and understand leadership.

The chair operates within a complex environment that requires a number of **roles** to be filled. The most important of these roles are:

- planner;
- motivator;
- information disseminator; and,
- facilitator.

117

The most significant outcome to be accomplished is the creation of a positive work environment, and the chair achieves this through a variety of specific **tasks**. On any given day, the chair may be involved with any or all of the following crucial tasks:

- communicate needs to upper level administrators, and from administration to unit faculty;
- address tasks related to faculty: recruit, select, provide feedback, and encourage professional development;
- update the curriculum and courses;
- set personal and professional goals; and,
- develop long-range unit plans, and integrate them with institutional plans.

There are numerous **skills** which the chair would identify as being important, with very little distinction between which are most vital. The five most important skills are:

- sensitivity: the ability to deal with people;
- judgement: the ability to reach logical conclusions and make high quality decisions;
- organization: the ability to deal with a volume of paperwork and heavy time demands;
- leadership: ability to recognize when a group requires direction; and,
- decisiveness: ability to recognize when a decision is required.

The community college department chair will face a number of **challenges** in the coming five years. The most pressing of these challenges are:

- maintaining program quality;
- maintaining high quality faculty who employ new teaching techniques;
- strengthening the curriculum and changing it in response to technological developments;
- responding to the needs of a wider range of students;
- meeting varied technological demands including securing and maintaining state-of-the-art equipment, increasing the use of computer technology in the classroom, and keeping pace with technology's increasing costs; and,
- obtaining financial resources while addressing accountability issues.

To deal with these challenges, the chair will plan to make use of several key **strategies**:

- conduct curriculum reviews to maintain relevance;
- balance personal and professional activities;
- network with other chairs, and assess personal professional development needs as a chair;
- assess future employment trends and opportunities;

- develop long-range institutional plans and integrate unit plans within the institutional framework;
- enhance staff development programs; and,
- utilize advising councils for input about a wide range of issues and topics.

Discussion

In this section, an analysis is made of the implications related to leadership development, and policy and structure.

Leadership Development

Given the importance of the chair position, chairs should be the major focus of leadership development.

Chairs must be prepared to transform the unit and this can be accomplished through searching, self-examination, reflective thinking and development. Leadership can be developed through a variety of means (see Seagren et al., 1993; McDade & Green, 1991; McDade, 1987). Chairs should assertively seek out a variety of situations within their institution (networking with other chairs and higher-level administrators, reading, workshops, retreats, conferences, seminars, and the development of individualized professional development plans) as well as utilize the various regional, national, and international opportunities available (disciplinary conferences with chair sessions, chair-focused conferences, workshops on topics of particular interest and need, as well as networking with chairs on other campuses). These experiences should address both long-term and short-term needs and interests of the chair, unit and campus.

Beyond the opportunities to learn directly from people through conferences, workshops and networks, chairs should become aware of and use the wealth of written material available to them. Two useful and well researched series are the ASHE-ERIC monographs published by George Washington University, and The New Directions series in the areas of Teaching and Learning, Institutional Research, Higher Education, and Adult and Continuing Education, all from Jossey-Bass Publications. Both Jossey-Bass and Onyx Press (formerly ACE-Macmillan) produce a set of leadership/management and institutional development materials that are also quite readable and well reviewed. There are also a number of newsletters that provide useful ideas, information and strategies for chairs. In the near future, electronic network possibilities for addressing chair issues can be expected (e.g., through the National Community College Chair Academy).

119

Chairs must participate in active learning activities (e.g., Institute for Academic Leadership Development Practicum) and make journaling and reflection part of regular professional practice. Work by Argyris (1993) and Schön (1983) are particularly helpful in realizing that intentions and actions are controlled by the frameworks of personal experience. To move beyond personal experience requires working through and gaining new insights about situations in which better decisions could have been made.

In their comments and responses, chairs indicate their desire to be leaders as well as managers. They do not just want to maintain the status quo or do things right, they want to be significant players in deciding what should be done ("doing the right things") to transform the unit.

Using the proposed model of the department chair described in Chapter One (**Figure 1.1**), leadership development can be related to the various components of the framework identified: personal characteristics, responsibilities, challenges and response strategies.

Personal Characteristics

Faculty and other individuals interested in becoming chairs should make opportunities to identify and analyze the degree of congruence of their qualifications, beliefs and aspirations in relationship to the profiles presented in this research. Institutions should provide opportunities for potential chairs to have increasing leadership responsibilities through committee assignments and short-term administrative assignments so that chair prospects will have an opportunity to test their interests, abilities, and skills.

Responsibilities, roles, tasks, and skills are dimensions that every chair should address in developing effectiveness. Since several roles were perceived as important by virtually all chairs, priority should be given to development of planner, motivator, information disseminator, and facilitator roles. Others, such as advocate and mentor, may be roles which can evolve through experiential learning in faculty assignments, and be enhanced by workshops and practice. Others may require building from the fundamentals; for example, the evaluator role requires a conceptual framework and set of skills which can be learned and practiced. Institutions can encourage chairs to take advantage of the learning opportunities and encourage networking with experienced chairs to build upon and develop any of these roles.

A number of chair tasks were identified as important. The seven task clusters (**Table 6.2**) provide a useful framework for organizing how chairs can formulate learning strategies in these areas. For example, the *Budget Tasks* cluster is composed of: prepare unit budgets, monitor unit budgets and allocate resources to priority activities. Even though some budgeting principles can be learned through external workshops and reading, much needs to be learned in the specific institutional context. Networking with other chairs or administrators who develop and implement budgets can be most useful. The task clusters can be analyzed by the chairs, and strategies and activities identified to increase effectiveness and efficiency for any of the tasks.

Skills encompassed in the *Administrative Skills and Leadership* and *Interpersonal Skills* clusters (**Table 7.2**) were identified as important. Several are primarily conceptual skills, requiring the ability and perspective to understand how the individual parts relate to the good of the whole (see Katz & Henry, 1988). Use of structured activities such as those offered by the NASSP Assessment Center have demonstrated effectiveness in assessing and developing administrator skills. Institutions should encourage the use of these experiences or encourage the development regionally or nationally of an assessment battery focused on the chair position.

Interpersonal skills were also identified as crucial to the chair position. Since communication is critical to most organizational functions (planning, meetings, conferencing, delegating), chairs should seek out opportunities to increase their abilities in this area. Focused communication skill building sessions can be useful, as well as designing activities which provide opportunities for people to interact with new and different groups. Institutions can encourage chairs to take advantage of these experiences, both internally and externally.

The chairs identified a number of challenges as important. In terms of leadership development, many of the challenges require a high level of understanding, some of which can be acquired through reading and analysis with effective coaching and mentoring from higher level administrators and peers. Institutions can also use content experts and consultants to aid in analysis and response to these challenges.

Chairs identified a range of strategies to address the challenges. Four strategy clusters identified were: *Chair Development, Planning, Personal and Professional Development*, and *External and Financial* (**Table 9.2**). The chair development strategies provide a set of activities to help people prepare for and continue to develop in the position. The other three clusters provide strategies that focus on planning, development of others and external and financial strategies. Institutions can provide opportunities through workshops and training events for chairs to use and develop these strategies.

Institutional Commitment

Institutions can provide structure and policies that encourage effective chair leadership. Although each of the chapters include some specific implications, some of the more important are restated or reformulated here as summary statements.

Chairs should be seen as a part of the administrative team with support and open communication with everyone on the team. Teams should provide opportunities for all members to enhance leadership and to practice a repertoire of behaviors.

Institutions should clarify their expectations of chairs and provide opportunities for chairs to develop their leadership effectiveness through preparation for the position and other experiences. Professional development activities should encourage on-going participation in policy formulation and decision-making by chairs and prospective chairs, and funds should be allotted so individuals can take advantage of the activities.

With increased importance being attached to the establishment of leadership continuity, institutions must carefully think through how they will address major turnovers in the chair positions in the coming years. While some characteristics of the present chair profile may be important in the selection of future chairs, there may be other aspects to consider. For example, if institutions desire to have greater participation of women and minorities, they will need to identify and groom individuals for these positions as well as describe what skills and abilities are important in the future. The present chairs understand the culture and mission of the community college because they have been faculty members. If chairs are appointed in the future without this background, careful consideration will need to be given to orientation and other developmental activities focused on a range of issues to create an understanding of community colleges.

Since chairs are expected to provide leadership as well as management, position descriptions should reflect and describe expectations and responsibilities for both areas. Institutions may want to encourage and provide opportunities to develop transformational leadership (Bass & Avolio, 1993) and reflective leadership (see Argyris, 1993; Schön, 1983). Both are important and necessary to develop the kind of perspective necessary to deal with the challenges of the information age.

Institutional development activities should provide for both short- and long-term involvement. Use of individually developed professional development plans by chairs can provide the structure and accountability to address continuous improvement so essential for quality.

Institutions should reward and recognize chairs for participating in development programs and for reaching out into new dimensions of leadership. Participation in these activities should be taken into account in performance evaluations, salary increases and promotions.

Since organizational understanding and skills (planning, curriculum development, and budgeting) and human relations understanding and skills (mentoring and conflict resolution) are both necessary for leadership success, institutions should encourage development at both of these levels. The chair is constantly confronted with situations requiring both sets of skills, and lack of competence in either can lead to ineffectiveness. Institutions should conduct periodic checks to ensure that they are providing the range of activities to meet these needs.

Given the continuing challenges faced by chairs (Seagren et al., 1993), institutional policies and activities should encourage long-range planning and discussion as well as addressing immediate needs. Activities that can move chairs forward include challenging reading, open dialogues, and retreats.

As institutions respond to the demands of quality assurance, they should continually search for methods and perspectives that keep them "user friendly" with their clientele and on a journey of continuous improvement. Adopting and implementing relevant principles of Total Quality Management can provide some of the necessary structure. Chairs must be familiar and capable of dealing with the full range of quality and accountability issues.

Future Research Agenda

This study developed a national profile of community college chairpersons. To date, no other study of chairpersons, either for two-year college or four-year institutions, has undertaken such an expansive data collection effort. How, then, can this data be utilized to establish a clearer vision of chairs and to provide an understanding of areas that surfaced from the implications in the present study? Below are mentioned several topics worthy of further study:

• This project identified skills, tasks, and roles of present chairs. Performance levels were not investigated, and left to further research is whether chairs are presently excelling, or operating at another level of competency. What are some factors that help explain why one chair would be proficient at certain skills tasks and roles and another chair less proficient? How do chairs achieve competency? The entire area of exploring excellence and competence as a chair remains open for study.

• This study examined only the chair, not other members of the leadership teams on community college campuses. For example, instructional deans and presidents provide leadership that must be translated into action by chairs. Further

123

examination of the roles, skills, tasks, and challenges of deans and presidents and how the leadership team functions in the community college is required. Further, how does an instructional dean or president view the leadership abilities of chairs? What criteria would they (or do they) use to evaluate chairs? What rewards exist for chairs and how are they recognized by their supervisors for excellent performances? What are the characteristics of the working relationship between chairs and other members of the team? Answers to these questions will illuminate further the leadership aspects of chairs within the campus context in which they work.

• This study focused heavily on the need for leadership development for chairs. How should leadership development occur? What should be the balance between development activities that are conducted and sponsored in-house versus those that are available through national and regional workshops? What levels of leadership development are now occurring? What types are most prevalent and effective? How many chairs participate and to what degree? How much institutional support exists or should exist for development activities?

• As a result of the study, the demographic characteristics of existing chairs are now well defined. As the year 2000 approaches, a reliable projection of the turnover of chairs needs to be made. What must be done to systematically determine future needs and plans? What can be done to recruit more minorities to more accurately reflect the national population characteristics anticipated for the year 2000? In selecting individuals for chair positions, how much importance should be given to experience in the selection and promotion process as opposed to participation in development activities? What would be the impact of recruiting chairs from other than the faculty ranks? What impact will the recruitment of chairs from the faculty ranks have on the make-up and composition of the faculty? These are a few of the demographic and characteristic issues that need further exploration.

• The study involved responses received only from the chair perspective. Since chairs work within a larger context of the campus, what are faculty views about the work of chairs? Do faculty feel that chairs need further "leadership development?" Do faculty concur with the priorities given to tasks, skills, roles, challenges, and strategies by chairs? To obtain an accurate reading on the work of chairs, further study of those with whom they have significant interaction on campus will be necessary.

• Chairs confirmed the heavy reliance on part-time faculty in the delivery of instructional programs in community colleges. There are many advantages such as increased flexibility of staffing, hiring individuals with considerable skill and expertise, and reduced cost for staffing through the use of part-time faculty. Still a number of topics need to be researched in relation to their use. What strategies can chairs utilize to effectively bring part-time faculty into the mainstream of the organization's mission, procedures, and processes? What are the special types of developmental activities chairs need to provide for part-time faculty in terms of course syllabus development, teaching techniques and procedures, student evaluations, and relationships to business and industry? What changes need to be made in faculty evaluation procedures to accommodate part-time faculty?

• The nature of community colleges is changing due to the increase in academic transfer programs and the development of tech-prep programs. Therefore, a number of issues need to be researched. How can a sense of community and institutional commitment from both academic transfer and vocational/technical oriented faculty be built? What are the implications of the "seamless web" or 2+2+2 concepts for articulation with secondary schools and four-year institutions? What are the implications of the open admission policies for academic transfer programs? What impact will the trend toward outcome-based education and competencies at the secondary education levels have on admission standards for the community colleges?

• The availability and use of technology will have an impact on all types of educational institutions, but particularly on the community college. Therefore, the chair must consider the following issues or topics. How should the programs and curriculum of community colleges be changed to take advantage of the available instructional technology? How will new distance learning strategies impact both academic transfer and vocational programs? What type and level of student competency in the use of technology should be required for admission? What faculty development activities need to be developed and provided to prepare faculty to capitalize on the advantages of the available technology?

• There will be significant changes in the relationship of formal to informal faculty and leadership development programs. How do formal graduate leadership programs need to be adapted or modified to meet the demand of chairs for the skills required to function effectively? What type of partnerships can be developed between two- and four-year graduate schools for developing academic leadership development programs?

• As the community colleges gain status as viable players in the delivery of postsecondary education, two important organizational questions need to be researched. Can these colleges retain their spirit of entrepreneurship and remain responsive to community needs after the growth period is over? Will a balance be maintained between two different instructional foci of campuses? What needs to be done to assure that appropriate recognition is given and maintained for the vocational technical oriented programs and faculty?

The data developed from this survey and results obtained from further research will provide useful information for decision-making about community colleges in the future. The time is right; challenges exist and effective academic leaders can capitalize on these to transform community colleges into what they need and should be to prepare students for the 21st century. Chairs will need to be involved in marketing efforts to a largely uninformed public, and in expanding and enhancing linkages and partnerships with the community, business and industry. The issues of quality and accountability will require the chair to be skilled in assessing outcomes. Finally, chairs must create a vision for the unit, empower faculty, and build consensus. These opportunities make the position of chair an exciting one worthy of the best in leadership development programs.

References

Adelman. (1992). The way we are: The community college as American thermometer. Washington, DC: U.S. Department of Education.

Albright, M. J., & Graf, D. L. (Eds.). (1992). Teaching in the information age: The role of educational technology. New Directions for Teaching and Learning, 51. San Francisco: Jossey-Bass.

Argyris, C. (1993). Knowledge for action: A guide to overcoming barriers to organizational change. San Francisco: Jossey-Bass.

Bass, B. M. (1985). Leadership and performance beyond expectations. New York: The Free Press.

Bass, B. M., & Avolio, B. J. (1993). Improving organizational effectiveness through transformational leadership. Three Oaks, CA: Sage.

Belenky, M. F., Clinchy, B. M., Goldberger, N. R., & Tarule, J. M. (1989). Women's ways of knowing. New York: Basic Books.

Bennett, J. B., & Figuli, D. J. (1990). Enhancing departmental leadership: The roles of the chairperson. New York: American Council on Education/Macmillan.

Bennis, W. G., & Nanus, B. (1985). Leaders: The strategies for taking charge. New York: Harper & Row.

Birnbaum, R. (1988). How colleges work. San Francisco: Jossey-Bass.

Boice, R. (1992). Lessons learned about mentoring. In M. D. Sorcinelli & A. E. Austin (Eds.), Developing new and junior faculty. New Directions for Teaching and Learning, 50, pp. 51-61. San Francisco: Jossey-Bass.

Booth, D. B. (1982). The department chair: Professional development and role conflict. (ASHE-ERIC Higher Education Research Report. No. 10). Washington, DC: American Association for Higher Education.

Bowen, H. R. (1980). The cost of higher education: How much do colleges and universities spend per student and how much should they spend? San Francisco: Jossey-Bass.

Boyer, E. L. (1987). College: The undergraduate experience in America. New York: Harper & Row.

Brass, R. (Ed.). (1984). Community colleges, the future and SPOD. Stillwater, OK: New Forums Press.

Brint, S., & Karabel, J. (1989). The diverted dream: Community colleges and the promise of educational opportunity in America, 1900-1985. New York: Oxford University.

Broadway, D. M. (1984). The role of the department or division chairperson in the public junior colleges of Mississippi. Doctoral dissertation, The University of Mississippi.

Campbell, H. W. (1988). The value and meaning of general education to electronic technician students as perceived by electronic chairpersons at selected California community colleges. Doctoral dissertation, University of Southern California.

Carnegie Foundation for the Advancement of Teaching. (1989). The condition of the professoriate: Attitudes and trends, 1989: A technical report. Princeton, NJ: Author.

Carroll, J. B., & Gmelch, W. H. (1992). The relationship of department chair roles to importance of chair duties. Paper presented at the Annual Meeting of the Association for the Study of Higher Education, Minneapolis, MN.

Chaffee, E. E., & Sherr, L. A. (1992). Quality: Transforming postsecondary education (ASHE-ERIC Higher Education Report No. 3). Washington, DC: The George Washington University, School of Education and Human Development.

Cohen, A. M., & Brawer, F. B. (1989). The American Community College. San Francisco: Jossey-Bass.

Cope, R. G. (1987). Opportunity from strength: Strategic planning clarified with case examples. (ASHE-ERIC Higher Education Report No. 8). Washington, DC: Association for the Study of Higher Education.

Covey, S. R. (1991). Principle-centered leadership. New York: Summit Books.

Creswell, J., Wheeler, D., Seagren, A., Egly, N., & Beyer, K. (1990). The academic chairperson's handbook. Lincoln, NE: University of Nebraska Press.

Crocker, L. & Algina, J. (1986). Introduction to classical and modern test theory. New York: Holt, Rinehart, and Winston.

Cross, K. P., & Fideler, E. F. (1989). Community college missions: Priorities in the mid-1980's. Journal of Higher Education, 60, 209-216.

Deegan, W. L., Tillery, D. & Melone, R. J. (1985). The process of renewal: An agenda for action. In W. L. Deegan & D. Tillery (Eds.), Renewing the American community college: Priorities and strategies for effective leadership. San Francisco: Jossey-Bass.

Dewey, J. (1963). Experience and education. New York: Collier Books.

Drucker, P. F. (1974). Management: Tasks, responsibilities, practices (1st ed.). New York: Harper & Row.

Eaton, J. (1992). The coming transformation of community colleges. Planning for Higher Education, 21(1), 1-7.

Eble, K. (1986). Chairpersons and faculty development. The Department Advisor, 1, 1-5.

El-Khawas, E. (1991). Senior faculty in academe: Active, committed to the teaching role. ACE Research Briefs, 2(5), 1-12.

Ferguson, J. J. (1993). The complex role of the department chair or little wheels make the world go around. Paper presented at the 2nd International Conference for Community College Chairs and Deans, Phoenix, AZ.

Foster, R. (1992). Professional educator's meeting: Summary report. Battle Creek, MI: W. K. Kellogg Foundation.

French, J. B. (1980). An analysis of the role and professional development needs of the first-line administrators in the technical community colleges of Nebraska. Unpublished doctoral dissertation, University of Nebraska-Lincoln.

Fruchter, B. (1954). Introduction to factor analysis. New York: D. Van Nostrand.

Gappa, J. M., & Leslie, D. W. (1993). The invisible faculty: Improving the status of part-timers in higher education. San Francisco: Jossey-Bass.

Garms, W. I. (1977). Financing community colleges. New York: Teachers College, Columbia University.

Gilligan, C. (1982). In a different voice. Cambridge, MA: Harvard University Press.

Gmelch, W., & Burns, J. S. (1991). Sources of stress for academic department chairs: A national perspective. Paper presented at a meeting of the American Educational Research Association, Chicago, IL.

Gmelch, W. H., & Miskin, V. D. (1993). Leadership skills for department chairs. Bolton, MA: Anker

Goldenberg, M. (1990). Common and uncommon concerns: The complex role of the community college department chair. In J. B. Bennett & D. J. Figuli (Eds.), Enhancing departmental leadership: The roles of the chairperson. New York: America Council on Education/Macmillan.

Green, M., & McDade, S. (1991). Investing in higher education: A handbook of leadership development. New York: ACE/Macmillan.

Hammons, J. O., & Wallace, T. H. S. (1977). Staff development needs of public community college department/division chairpersons. Community/Junior College Research Quarterly, 2, 55-76.

Hawthorne, E., & Ninke, D. (1990). A focus on university faculty service to community colleges. Community College Review, 19(1), 30-35.

Helgesen, S. (1990). The female advantage: Women's ways of leadership. New York: Doubleday/Currency.

Hinkle, D. E., Wiersma, W., & Jurs, S. G. (1988). Applied statistics for the behavioral sciences (2nd ed.). Boston: Houghton Mifflin.

Holly, M. L. (1984). Keeping a personal-professional journal. ESA 843 School-based professional development, (28-43). Victoria 3217, Australia: Deakin University Press.

Jennerich, E. J. (1981). Competencies for department chairpersons: Myths and realities. Liberal Education, 67(1), 46-70.

Johnson, M. (1991). A survey of factors affecting workplace performance and career advancement of black women administrators in middle and upper level management positions in community colleges. Paper presented at Leadership 2000, Chicago, IL.

Kaikai, S. M., & Kaikai, R. E. (1990). Chairpersons as promoters of community service. Maryland: Catonsville Community College. (ERIC Document Reproduction Service No. ED 321 801).

Katz, J., & Henry, M. (1988). Turning professors into teachers: A new approach to faculty development and student learning. New York: ACE/Macmillan.

Kimmons, W. J. (1977). Black administrators in public community colleges: Self-perceived role and status. New York: Carlton Press.

Lamb, B. (1993). Promoting excellent teaching: The chair as academic leader. Paper presented at the 2nd International Conference for Community College Chairs, Deans, and Other Instructional Leaders, Phoenix, AZ.

Likins, P. (1990, May). In an era of tight budgets and public criticism, colleges must rethink their goals and priorities. Chronicle of Higher Education, 36, B1-B2.

Lunde, J. P., & Hartung, T. (1990). Integrating individual and organizational needs. In J. H. Schuster & D. W. Wheeler (Eds.), Enhancing faculty careers: Strategies for development and renewal. San Francisco: Jossey-Bass.

Lunde, J. P., Wheeler, D. W., Hartung, T., & Wheeler, B. J. (1991). Second order change: Impact of a college renewal program over time. Innovative Higher Education, 16(2), 125-138.

Maehr, M. L., & Braskamp, L. A. (1986). The motivation factor. Lexington, MA: Lexington.

McDade, S. A. (1987). Higher education leadership: Enhancing skills through professional development programs. (Report No. 5). Washington, DC: Association for the Study of Higher Education. (ERIC Document Reproduction Service No. ED 293 479).

McLaughlin, G. W., Montgomery, J. R., & Malpass, L. F. (1975). Selected characteristics, roles, goals, and satisfactions of department chairmen in state and land-grant institutions. Research in Higher Education, 3, 243-259.

McNulty, L. J. (1980). The nature of selected group dynamics operating within faculty committees at the University of Nebraska-Lincoln. Unpublished master's thesis, University of Nebraska-Lincoln, Lincoln, NE.

Menschenfreund, R. (1993). The role of the instructional dean and associate dean in the community college: An institutional study. Hastings, NE: Central Community College.

Miller, M. T., & Seagren, A. T. (1992). Faculty leader perceptions of improving participation in higher education governance. College Student Journal, 27(1), 112-118.

Miller, M., Edmunds, N., & Mahler, M. (1992, November). Developing the higher and vocational education partnership: Priorities for the next decade. Resources in Education (ERIC Clearinghouse on Adult, Career, and Vocational Education Reproduction Service No. ED 346 344).

Mooney, C. J. (1992). Critics within and without academe assail professors at research universities. The Chronicle of Higher Education, 39(10), A17.

Moore, K. M., Twombly, S. B., & Martorana, S. V. (1985). Today's academic leaders: A national study of administrators in community and junior colleges. University Park: Center for the Study of Higher Education, Pennsylvania State University.

Morrison, A. M. (1992). The new leaders: Guidelines on leadership diversity in America. San Francisco: Jossey-Bass.

Moses, I., & Roe, E. (1990). Heads and chairs: Managing academic departments. St. Lucia, Queensland, Australia: University of Queensland Press.

Murray, J. P. (1992). The department chairperson: The confessions of a researcher turned practitioner. Paper presented at the National Conference on Successful College Teaching and Administration, Orlando, FL.

Nanus, B. (1992). Visionary leadership. San Francisco: Jossey-Bass.

NASSP. (1992). Personal communication from Paul W. Hersey, Director of Professional Assistance, The National Association of Secondary School Principals, September 3, 1992.

Norton, M.S. (1980). Academic department chair: Tasks and responsibilities. Tempe, AZ: The Department of Educational Administration and Supervision.

Palmer, P., Wheeler, B. G., & Fowler, J. W. (Eds.). (1990). Caring for the commonweal: Education for religious and public life. Macon, GA: Mercer University Press.

Parnell, D. (1990). Dateline 2000: The new higher education agenda. Washington, DC: The Community College Press.

Peltason, J. W. (1984). Foreword. In A. Tucker (Ed.), Chairing the academic department: Leadership among peers. New York: American Council on Education/MacMillan.

Riggs, R. O., & Akor, M. F. (1992). Strategic planning in the community college: Role of academic department and division chairpersons. Community/Junior College Quarterly, 16, 57-75.

Roach, J. H. L. (1976). The academic department chairperson: Roles and responsibilities. Educational Record, 57(1), 13-23.

Roueche, J. E., Baker, G. A., & Rose, R. R. (1989). Shared vision: Transformational leadership in American community colleges. Washington, DC: The Community College Press.

Roueche, J. E., & Roueche, S. D. (1993). Between a rock and a hard place: The at-risk student in the open door college. Washington, DC: American Association of Community Colleges.

Schön, D. (1983). The reflective practitioner: How professionals think in action. New York: Basic.

Schuster, J. H., & Wheeler, D. W. (1990). Enhancing faculty careers: Strategies for development and renewal. San Francisco: Jossey-Bass.

Scott, J. H. (1990). Role of community college department chairs in faculty development. Community College Review, 18(3), 12-16.

Seagren, A. T. (1978). Perceptions of administrative tasks and professional development needs by chairpersons of academic departments: A questionnaire. Lincoln, NE: University of Nebraska-Lincoln, Office of the Assistant Vice Chancellor for Program Development and Review, Task Force on Management Practices in Higher Education.

Seagren, A., Creswell, J., & Wheeler, D. (1993). The department chair: New roles, responsibilities, and challenges (ASHE-ERIC Higher Education Report No. 1). Washington, DC: The George Washington University, School of Education and Human Development.

Seagren, A., & Miller, M. (in press). Caught in the middle: The pressures of chairing an instructional unit. The Department Chair: A Newsletter for Academic Administrators. Bolton, MA: Anker.

Seagren, A., & Miller, M. (1994). Academic leaders and the community college: A North American profile. Academic Leadership: Journal of the National Community College Chair Academy, 1, 6-11.

Senge, P. M. (1990). The fifth discipline: The art and practice of the learning organization. New York: Doubleday.

Seymour, D. T. (1993). On Q: Causing quality in higher education. Phoenix: Onyx.

Simpson, W. M. (1984). Division heads and role strain perception. Community College Review, 12(1), 21-26.

Sirotnik, K., & Goodlad, J. (1988). School-university partnerships in action. Concepts, cases, and concerns. New York: Teachers College, Columbia University.

Smart, J. C., & Elton, C. F. (1976). Administrative roles of department chairmen. In J. C. Smart & J. R. Montgomery (Eds.), Examining departmental management. New Directions for Institutional Research, 2. San Francisco: Jossey-Bass.

Smart, J. C., & Montgomery, J. R. (Eds.). (1976). Examining departmental management. New Directions for Institutional Research, 10. San Francisco: Jossey-Bass.

Smith, R. M. (1992). Assessing faculty. In M. Hickson & D. W. Stacks (Eds.), Effective communication for academic chairs. (pp. 91-105). Albany, NY: State University of New York Press.

Smutek, M. M. (1988). An examination of the place of comprehensive liberal education: Curricular challenge for community colleges. Doctoral dissertation, University of Massachusetts.

Sorcinelli, M. D., & Austin, A. E. (Eds.). (1992). Developing new and junior faculty. New Directions for Teaching and Learning, 50. San Francisco: Jossey-Bass.

Spitzack, C. J. (1988). Rethinking the relationship between power, expression and research practices. In C. A. Valentine & N. Hoar (Eds.), Women and communicative power: Theory research and practice (pp. 118-125). Annandale, VA: Speech Communication Association.

Stacks, D. W. & Hickson, M. (1992). Appendix B: Providing information. In M. Hickson & D. W. Stacks (Eds.), <u>Effective communication for academic chairs</u>. Albany, NY: State University of New York Press.

Tucker, A. (1984). <u>Chairing the academic department: Leadership among peers</u> (2nd ed.). New York: American Council on Education/Macmillan.

Tucker, A. (1992). <u>Chairing the academic department: Leadership among peers</u> (3rd ed.). Phoenix, AZ: American Council on Education/Onyx.

Vavrus, L. G., Grady, M. L., & Creswell, J. W. (1988). The faculty development role of department chairs: A naturalistic analysis. <u>Planning and Changing</u>, <u>19</u>(1), 14-29.

Winner, C. A. (1989). <u>The role and function of the departmental chairperson at Delaware Technical and Community College</u>. Three executive position papers submitted to the faculty of the University of Delaware in partial fulfillment of the requirements for the degree of Doctor of Education in Educational Leadership, University of Delaware.

Wunsch, M. (Ed.). (in press). Mentoring revisited. <u>New Directions in Teaching and Learning</u>, <u>57</u>. San Francisco: Jossey-Bass.

Appendix A

The International Survey

A C A D E M Y

September 28, 1992

Dear Colleague,

This study is the first national survey of its kind and is being distributed to all community and junior college chairpersons (approximately 12,000 in two-year colleges) in the United States and Canada. This survey is being completed by chairs in all occupational and academic areas.

It is a ground-breaking effort to identify key professional data about chairpersons and it will form an essential international data base for future efforts to address concerns and provide professional training programs and services for chairs. Your input will help us better understand the complex role and responsibilities of this position. The American Association of Community and Junior Colleges and The National Community College Chair Academy encourage you to complete the enclosed survey about chairing an academic unit in community colleges.

As an individual holding the position of a "chair" or comparable position/title such as coordinator, director, associate dean, or head, we are asking that you spend the next twenty-five minutes completing this survey. In the survey when we refer to your academic unit, we mean your department, division, area or section - the unit you administer.

This survey does not contain sensitive information.˙ However, we have coded a number on the response form so that we can identify individuals who have responded. We can then send follow-up letters to those individuals who did not return the survey.

135

Question number 52 provides an opportunity for you to receive an abstract of the results from the survey. Information and results will be presented at the Second Annual Conference of Community College Chairs to be held February 17-20, 1993 in Phoenix, Arizona.

In advance, we thank you for your time and providing the Chair Academy with important information that will be used to help us in the design of training programs and services for community college chairs.

Please use the enclosed optical scan form to record your responses and mail it back in the enclosed, self addressed envelope. You do not need to return the survey. Please return the optical scan form by October 31, 1992.

Sincerely,

Gary Filan
Executive Director
The National Community College Chair Academy
(602) 461-7304

NATIONAL COMMUNITY COLLEGE CHAIR ACADEMY
1833 WEST SOUTHERN AVENUE, MESA, ARIZONA 85202
(602) 461-7304 FAX (602) 461-7806
SPONSORED BY THE MARICOPA COMMUNITY COLLEGES

INTERNATIONAL COMMUNITY COLLEGE CHAIR SURVEY 1992

National Community College Chair Academy

A C A D E M Y

Community College Chairperson Survey

Sponsored by The National Community College Chair Academy, Maricopa Community Colleges and The University of Nebraska-Lincoln

Gary Filan, Executive Director, The National Community College Chair Academy (602)461-7304

Alan T. Seagren, Director, Center for the Study of Higher and Postsecondary Education, University of Nebraska-Lincoln

Survey Researchers:

John W. Creswell, Professor
Educational Psychology
University of Nebraska-Lincoln

Lindsay J. Barker, Visiting Professor
Educational Administration
University of Nebraska-Lincoln

Michael T. Miller, Assistant Professor
Vocational and Adult Education
University of Nebraska-Lincoln

Daniel W. Wheeler, Associate Professor
Cooperative Extension Service
University of Nebraska-Lincoln

138

Community College Chairperson Survey

Directions

Please use a No. 2 pencil and mark your responses <u>only</u> on the machine-scorable response sheet. Darken the circle of your choice. No writing or marks should be made outside the circles. If you need to change responses, complete erase the first mark and fill in the circle with your new response.

As you complete this survey key terms are being utilized: "Chair" means comparable position/title such as coordinator, director, associate dean, or head. By "academic unit" we mean your department, division, area or section - the unit you administer.

Please note that certain responses to questions refer you to answer other questions, therefore depending on how you respond, you may be leaving certain questions/responses "blank" on your machine-scorable response sheet.

Characteristics of Your Instructional Unit:

1. Your present position:
    (1) Chair_____
    (2) Head_____
    (3) Both head and chair_____
    (4) Coordinator/Director_____
    (5) Asst/Assoc Dean_____
    (6) Other_____

2. Name of the instructional **unit** for which you are responsible:
    (1) Department_____
    (2) Division_____
    (3) Area_____
    (4) Specialization_____
    (5) Other_____

3. Student headcount (full + part-time) in your **unit**:
    (1) 200 or less_____
    (2) 201-400_____
    (3) 401-600_____
    (4) 601-800_____
    (5) 801-1000_____
    (6) Over 1000_____

4. Full-time faculty (headcount) in your **unit**:
   (1) 10 or less_____
   (2) 11-20_____
   (3) 21-30_____
   (4) 31-40_____
   (5) 41-50_____
   (6) Over 50_____

5. Part-time faculty (headcount) in your **unit**:
   (1) 10 or less_____
   (2) 11-20_____
   (3) 21-30_____
   (4) 31-40_____
   (5) 41-50_____
   (6) Over 50_____

6. Years your unit has been operating as an instructional **unit**:
   (1) Less than 1 year_____
   (2) 1-5 years_____
   (3) 6-10 years_____
   (4) 11-15 years_____
   (5) 16-20 years_____
   (6) More than 20 years_____

7. Indicate the type of degree most commonly conferred on graduates from your **unit:**

A. For **United States** units only:
   (1) Associate of Arts_____
   (2) Associate of Sciences_____
   (3) Associate of Applied Sciences_____
   (4) Associate of General Studies_____
   (5) Diploma or Certificate_____
   (6) Other_____

B. For **Canadian** units only:
   (1) Certificate_____
   (2) Diploma_____
   (3) Transfer program_____
   (4) B.A. degree_____
   (5) Other_____

140

8. Below are listed program areas in community colleges identified by the American Association of Community Colleges. Identify the program area with the **largest student enrollment** in your **unit**:
    - (1) Liberal Arts and Sciences_____
    - (2) General Studies_____
    - (3) Nursing/Allied Health_____
    - (4) Business Administration/Accounting_____
    - (5) Office/Business Support_____
    - (6) Engineering and Science Technology_____
    - (7) Education/Human Services_____
    - (8) Protective Services_____
    - (9) Agriculture and Natural Services_____
    - (10) Fine and Performing Arts_____
    - (11) Trades/Precision Production_____
    - (12) Sciences_____
    - (13) Computer Science Data Processing_____
    - (14) Personal Services_____
    - (15) Other_____

Characteristics of Your Campus

9. Number of **full-time** students (headcount) on your **campus**:
    - (1) 2000 or less_____
    - (2) 2001-4000_____
    - (3) 4001-6000_____
    - (4) 6001-8000_____
    - (5) 8001-10,000_____
    - (6) Over 10,000_____

10. Number of **part-time** students (headcount) on your **campus**:
    - (1) 2000 or less_____
    - (2) 2001-4000_____
    - (3) 4001-6000_____
    - (4) 6001-8000_____
    - (5) 8001-10,000_____
    - (6) Over 10,000_____

11. Number of **full-time** faculty (headcount) on your **campus**:
    (1) 50 or less_____
    (2) 51-100_____
    (3) 101-150_____
    (4) 151-200_____
    (5) 201-250_____
    (6) Over 250_____

12. Number of **part-time** faculty (headcount) on your **campus**:
    (1) 50 or less_____
    (2) 51-100_____
    (3) 101-150_____
    (4) 151-200_____
    (5) 201-250_____
    (6) Over 250_____

13. The number of chairpersons (or comparable position) on your **campus**:
    (1) 5 or less_____
    (2) 6-10_____
    (3) 11-20_____
    (4) 21-30_____
    (5) 31-40_____
    (6) More than 41_____

14. Answer this question **only** if your campus is a U.S. institution.
    Accrediting region where your campus is located:
    (1) New England_____
    (2) Middle States_____
    (3) Southern_____
    (4) North Central_____
    (5) Northwest_____
    (6) Western_____

15. The instructional focus of your campus:
    (1) Occupational/Technical_____
    (2) Academic Transfer_____
    (3) Both Technical and Transfer_____
    (4) Other_____

142

16. The primary source of your funding:
    (1) Public_____
    (2) Private_____ **(If you chose "Private," go to Question #20.)**

17. If public, degree of funding support from the State or Province:
    (1) 33% or less_____
    (2) 34% to 66%_____
    (3) 67% or more_____

18. If public, degree of funding support from the County/Region:
    (1) 33% or less_____
    (2) 34% to 66%_____
    (3) 67% or more_____

19. If public, degree of funding support from local/city:
    (1) 33% or less_____
    (2) 34% to 66%_____
    (3) 67% or more_____

20. The individual or group responsible for appointing/electing department or division chairs (or comparable position) after the search process on your campus:
    (1) Elected by faculty_____
    (2) Appointed by administration_____
    (3) Combination of faculty/administration_____
    (4) Other_____

Personal Information

21. Your age:
    (1) Under 30_____
    (2) 30-44_____
    (3) 45-54_____
    (4) 55-64_____
    (5) 65 and over_____

143

22. Your gender:
    (1) Female_____
    (2) Male_____

23. Your race:
    (1) Native American, Canadian Aleut, Eskimo, Inuit_____
    (2) Asian or Pacific Islander (Japanese, Chinese, Filipino, Asian Indian, Korean, Vietnamese, Hawaiian, Guamanian, Samoan, other Asian)_____
    (3) Black/African American_____
    (4) White_____
    (5) Hispanic/Latino_____
    (6) Other_____

24. Number of years of **your** professional experience working in community colleges as a **faculty member**:
    (1) 1-5 years_____
    (2) 6-10 years_____
    (3) 11-15 years_____
    (4) 16-20 years_____
    (5) Over 20 years_____
    (6) No experience_____

25. Number of years of **your** professional experience working in community colleges as a **chair or head** (or comparable position):
    (1) 1-5 years_____
    (2) 6-10 years_____
    (3) 11-15 years_____
    (4) 16-20 years_____
    (5) Over 20 years_____
    (6) No experience_____

26. Number of years of **your** professional experience working in community colleges in **other administrative positions**:
    (1) 1-5 years_____
    (2) 6-10 years_____
    (3) 11-15 years_____
    (4) 16-20 years_____
    (5) Over 20 years_____
    (6) No experience_____

27. Do you have prior experience working in business/industry?
    (1) Yes_____
    (2) No_____

28. Do you have prior experience working in 4-year colleges?
    (1) Yes_____
    (2) No_____

29. Do you have prior experience working in K-12 schools?
    (1) Yes_____
    (2) No_____

30. Do you have prior experience working in public agencies (e.g., government agencies)?
    (1) Yes_____
    (2) No_____

31. Do you have prior experience working in a university or professional school?
    (1) Yes_____
    (2) No_____

32. Do you have prior experience working in a vocational/technical college or institute?
    (1) Yes_____
    (2) No_____

33. Is your appointment as chair or head (or comparable position) limited to a specific term?
    (1) Yes_____
    (2) No_____ **(If you chose "No", go to Question #36.)**

34. If yes, length of the term:
    (1) Less than 3 years_____
    (2) 3 years_____
    (3) More than 3 years_____

35. If yes, is the appointment renewable?
    (1) Yes_____
    (2) No_____

36. Do you receive reassigned or released time from teaching for being a chair?
    (1)   Yes_____
    (2)   No_____   **(If you chose "No", go to Question #38.)**

37. If yes, how much time is reassigned or released in terms of 3-credit hour semester or quarter courses?
    (1)   1 class_____
    (2)   2 classes_____
    (3)   3 classes_____
    (4)   4 classes_____
    (5)   5 classes_____
    (6)   Full time_____

38. Do you receive a stipend for being a chair or head (or comparable position)?
    (1)   Yes_____
    (2)   No_____   **(If you chose "No", go to Question #40.)**

39. If yes, how much (on an annual basis)?
    (1) $500 or less_____
    (2) $501-1000_____
    (3) $1001-1500_____
    (4) $1501-2000_____
    (5) $2001-2500_____
    (6)   Over $2500_____

40. Your annual salary:
    (1) $20,000 or less_____
    (2) $21,000-40,000_____
    (3) $41,000-60,000_____
    (4) $61,000-80,000_____
    (5)   Over $80,000_____

41. Average number of hours you work in a typical week as a chair or head (or comparable position):
    (1)   10 or less_____
    (2)   11-20_____
    (3)   21-30_____
    (4)   31-40_____
    (5)   41-50_____
    (6)   50-60_____

42. Highest academic degree you have achieved:
    (1)   Less than baccalaureate_____
    (2)   Baccalaureate_____
    (3)   Masters_____
    (4)   Specialist Certificate/Degree_____
    (5)   Doctorate_____

43. Your professional plans in the next five years:
    (1)   Stay at the same community college_____
    (2)   Move to another community college_____
    (3)   Move to a 4-year institution of higher education_____
    (4)   Move to a position in the non-profit, private sector_____
    (5)   Retire_____
    (6)   Other_____

44. If you plan to **stay in community colleges**, what are your career plans for the next **five** years?
    (1)   Not applicable_____
    (2)   Remain in the chair position_____
    (3)   Move to a faculty position_____
    (4)   Move to another administrative position_____
    (5)   Other_____

45. If you plan to **move to another administrative position** at a community college, what is the position to which you aspire?
    (1)   Not applicable_____
    (2)   Dean_____
    (3)   Vice-president_____
    (4)   Campus president_____
    (5)   System chancellor_____
    (6)   Other_____

Educational Beliefs and Values

Please indicate the extent of your agreement or disagreement with each of the following statements. **Complete this sentence, "I place a high value on ..."** in terms of your current position in the unit.

		Strongly Agree	Agree	Neutral	Disagree	Strongly Disagree
46A.	General education	(1)	(2)	(3)	(4)	(5)
46B.	Occupational/technical education	(1)	(2)	(3)	(4)	(5)
46C.	Elective courses for students	(1)	(2)	(3)	(4)	(5)
46D.	Students gaining in-depth knowledge through a major	(1)	(2)	(3)	(4)	(5)
46E.	Values education incorporated into the curriculum	(1)	(2)	(3)	(4)	(5)
46F.	Opportunities for students to experience and understand leadership	(1)	(2)	(3)	(4)	(5)
46G.	Using computers in the classroom	(1)	(2)	(3)	(4)	(5)
46H.	An open admission policy for my department	(1)	(2)	(3)	(4)	(5)
46I.	An open admission policy for my college	(1)	(2)	(3)	(4)	(5)
46J.	Preparing students to meet the needs of the community	(1)	(2)	(3)	(4)	(5)
46K.	Encouraging faculty to use a wide variety of teaching approaches	(1)	(2)	(3)	(4)	(5)

Please indicate the extent of your agreement or disagreement with each of the following statements. **Complete this sentence, "I place a high value on ..."** in terms of your current position in the unit.

		Strongly Agree	Agree	Neutral	Disagree	Strongly Disagree
46L.	Promoting and encouraging the enrollment of minority students in the college	(1)	(2)	(3)	(4)	(5)
46M.	Preparing students to meet the needs of business/industry	(1)	(2)	(3)	(4)	(5)
46N.	Limiting the influence of accrediting agencies	(1)	(2)	(3)	(4)	(5)
46O.	Having selective admissions policies	(1)	(2)	(3)	(4)	(5)
46P.	Courses designed with open entry/open exit	(1)	(2)	(3)	(4)	(5)
46Q.	Students completing a degree program	(1)	(2)	(3)	(4)	(5)
46R.	The role of an advisory committee in establishing the curriculum	(1)	(2)	(3)	(4)	(5)
46S.	Training workers for specific companies	(1)	(2)	(3)	(4)	(5)
46T.	The concept of life-long learning	(1)	(2)	(3)	(4)	(5)
46U.	Student support services	(1)	(2)	(3)	(4)	(5)
46V.	Serving at-risk students	(1)	(2)	(3)	(4)	(5)

Please indicate the extent of your agreement or disagreement with each of the following statements. **Complete this sentence, "I place a high value on ..." in terms of your current position in the unit.**

		Strongly Agree	Agree	Neutral	Disagree	Strongly Disagree
46W.	Offering courses for limited English-speaking students	(1)	(2)	(3)	(4)	(5)
46X.	Providing development courses to students	(1)	(2)	(3)	(4)	(5)

Roles

How do you perceive your role as a chairperson? Indicate the degree of **importance** of each **role** to you in your current position:

		Very Important	Important	Undecided	Not Very Important	Not Important
47A.	Visionary	(1)	(2)	(3)	(4)	(5)
47B.	Motivator	(1)	(2)	(3)	(4)	(5)
47C.	Information disseminator	(1)	(2)	(3)	(4)	(5)

150

Cont'd	Roles

How do you perceive your role as a chairperson? Indicate the degree of **importance** of each **role** to you in your current position:

		Very Important	Important	Undecided	Not Very Important	Not Important
47D.	Resource allocator	(1)	(2)	(3)	(4)	(5)
47E.	Evaluator	(1)	(2)	(3)	(4)	(5)
47F.	Negotiator	(1)	(2)	(3)	(4)	(5)
47G.	Conflict resolver	(1)	(2)	(3)	(4)	(5)
47H.	Entrepreneur	(1)	(2)	(3)	(4)	(5)
47I.	Facilitator	(1)	(2)	(3)	(4)	(5)
47J.	Mentor	(1)	(2)	(3)	(4)	(5)
47K.	Delegator	(1)	(2)	(3)	(4)	(5)
47L.	Advocator	(1)	(2)	(3)	(4)	(5)
47M.	Caretaker	(1)	(2)	(3)	(4)	(5)
47N.	Planner	(1)	(2)	(3)	(4)	(5)

Below are listed tasks identified in the research literature as being performed by chairs or heads (or comparable position). Indicate the degree of **importance** of each task to you in your current position.

		Very Important	Important	Undecided	Not Very Important	Not Important
48A.	Conduct unit meetings	(1)	(2)	(3)	(4)	(5)
48B.	Create unit committees	(1)	(2)	(3)	(4)	(5)
48C.	Develop long-range unit plans	(1)	(2)	(3)	(4)	(5)
48D.	Prepare for accreditation	(1)	(2)	(3)	(4)	(5)
48E.	Create a positive work environment	(1)	(2)	(3)	(4)	(5)
48F.	Schedule classes	(1)	(2)	(3)	(4)	(5)
48G.	Update curriculum and courses	(1)	(2)	(3)	(4)	(5)
48H.	Recruit and select faculty	(1)	(2)	(3)	(4)	(5)
48I.	Assign faculty responsibilities	(1)	(2)	(3)	(4)	(5)
48J.	Evaluate faculty performance	(1)	(2)	(3)	(4)	(5)
48K.	Provide feedback to faculty	(1)	(2)	(3)	(4)	(5)
48L.	Terminate faculty	(1)	(2)	(3)	(4)	(5)
48M.	Recruit students	(1)	(2)	(3)	(4)	(5)
48N.	Advise and counsel students	(1)	(2)	(3)	(4)	(5)

Cont'd	Tasks

Below are listed tasks identified in the research literature as being performed by chairs or heads (or comparable position). Indicate the degree of **importance** of each task to you in your current position.

		Very Important	Important	Undecided	Not Very Important	Not Important
48O.	Prepare enrollment projections	(1)	(2)	(3)	(4)	(5)
48P.	Help students register	(1)	(2)	(3)	(4)	(5)
48Q.	Develop relationships with business and community groups	(1)	(2)	(3)	(4)	(5)
48R.	Communicate needs to upper-level administrators	(1)	(2)	(3)	(4)	(5)
48S.	Process paperwork and answer correspondence	(1)	(2)	(3)	(4)	(5)
48T.	Prepare unit budgets	(1)	(2)	(3)	(4)	(5)
48U.	Monitor unit budgets	(1)	(2)	(3)	(4)	(5)
48V.	Allocate resources to priority activities	(1)	(2)	(3)	(4)	(5)
48W.	Seek external funding	(1)	(2)	(3)	(4)	(5)
48X.	Supervise clerical/technical staff	(1)	(2)	(3)	(4)	(5)
48Y.	Maintain unit data bases	(1)	(2)	(3)	(4)	(5)
48Z.	Manage facilities and equipment	(1)	(2)	(3)	(4)	(5)

153

Cont'd	Tasks

Below are listed tasks identified in the research literature as being performed by chairs or heads (or comparable position). Indicate the degree of **importance** of each task to you in your current position:

		Very Important	Important	Undecided	Not Very Important	Not Important
48AA.	Set personal and professional goals	(1)	(2)	(3)	(4)	(5)
48BB.	Encourage the professional development of each faculty member	(1)	(2)	(3)	(4)	(5)
48CC.	Promote affirmative action	(1)	(2)	(3)	(4)	(5)
48DD.	Communicate information from administration to unit faculty	(1)	(2)	(3)	(4)	(5)
48EE.	Integrate unit plans with institutional plans	(1)	(2)	(3)	(4)	(5)
48FF.	Develop clerical/technical staff	(1)	(2)	(3)	(4)	(5)

Below are listed several skills. How **important** are these skills to you in your present position as chair or head (or comparable position)? (Skills adapted from the National Association of Secondary School Principals' Assessment Center Project.)

		Very Important	Important	Undecided	Not Very Important	Not Important
49A.	Problem analysis - Ability to seek out data and information to solve a problem	(1)	(2)	(3)	(4)	(5)
49B.	Judgement - Ability to reach logical conclusions and make high quality decisions	(1)	(2)	(3)	(4)	(5)
49C.	Organizational ability - Ability to be organized in dealing with a volume of paperwork and heavy demands on one's time	(1)	(2)	(3)	(4)	(5)
49D.	Decisiveness - Ability to recognize when a decision is required	(1)	(2)	(3)	(4)	(5)
49E.	Leadership - Ability to recognize when a group requires direction	(1)	(2)	(3)	(4)	(5)
49F.	Sensitivity - Ability to deal effectively with people	(1)	(2)	(3)	(4)	(5)
49G.	Stress tolerance - Ability to perform under pressure	(1)	(2)	(3)	(4)	(5)

Cont'd	Skills

Below are listed several skills. How **important** are these skills to you in your present position as chair or head (or comparable position)? (Skills adapted from the National Association of Secondary School Principals' Assessment Center Project.)

		Very Important	Important	Undecided	Not Very Important	Not Important
49H.	Oral communication - Ability to make a clear oral presentation	(1)	(2)	(3)	(4)	(5)
49I.	Written communication - Ability to express ideas clearly in writing	(1)	(2)	(3)	(4)	(5)
49J.	Range of interests - Ability to discuss a variety of societal issues	(1)	(2)	(3)	(4)	(5)
49K.	Personal motivation - Ability to show a need to achieve	(1)	(2)	(3)	(4)	(5)
49L.	Educational values - Ability to be receptive to new ideas and change	(1)	(2)	(3)	(4)	(5)

(Continued on next page)

Job Challenges

To what extent do you agree that the following are challenges you will have to face in your unit in the next **five years**:

		Strongly Agree	Agree	Neutral	Disagree	Strongly Disagree
50A	Changing the curriculum in response to technological development	(1)	(2)	(3)	(4)	(5)
50B.	Increasing general education requirements	(1)	(2)	(3)	(4)	(5)
50C.	Increasing human relations training	(1)	(2)	(3)	(4)	(5)
50D.	Internationalizing the curriculum	(1)	(2)	(3)	(4)	(5)
50E.	Keeping pace with the increasing cost of technology	(1)	(2)	(3)	(4)	(5)
50F.	Reallocating monies to programs because of financial constraints	(1)	(2)	(3)	(4)	(5)
50G.	Offering courses through distance education	(1)	(2)	(3)	(4)	(5)
50H.	Promoting greater gender equity	(1)	(2)	(3)	(4)	(5)
50I.	Accommodating cultural diversity	(1)	(2)	(3)	(4)	(5)
50J.	Decreasing growth in transfer programs	(1)	(2)	(3)	(4)	(5)
50K.	Encouraging more technical preparation in high schools	(1)	(2)	(3)	(4)	(5)

157

Cont'd	Job Challenges

To what extent do you agree that the following are challenges you will have to face in your unit in the next **five years**:

		Strongly Agree	Agree	Neutral	Disagree	Strongly Disagree
50L.	Securing and maintaining state-of-the-art technical equipment	(1)	(2)	(3)	(4)	(5)
50M.	Increasing influence and impact of state coordinating bodies	(1)	(2)	(3)	(4)	(5)
50N.	Increasing influence and impact of accrediting bodies	(1)	(2)	(3)	(4)	(5)
50O.	Increasing the use of business and industry advisory committees	(1)	(2)	(3)	(4)	(5)
50P.	Increasing teaching programs sponsored by specific companies	(1)	(2)	(3)	(4)	(5)
50Q.	Increasing involvement of the U.S. Government in establishing work conditions in colleges	(1)	(2)	(3)	(4)	(5)
50R.	Adapting to employees who utilize electronic communication systems and who work at home	(1)	(2)	(3)	(4)	(5)
50S.	Increasing the use of computers in the classroom	(1)	(2)	(3)	(4)	(5)
50T.	Responding to the needs of a wider range of students	(1)	(2)	(3)	(4)	(5)

Cont'd	Job Challenges

To what extent do you agree that the following are challenges you will have to face in your unit in the next **five years**:

		Strongly Agree	Agree	Neutral	Disagree	Strongly Disagree
50U.	Obtaining financial resources	(1)	(2)	(3)	(4)	(5)
50V.	Attracting new student populations	(1)	(2)	(3)	(4)	(5)
50W.	Maintaining program quality	(1)	(2)	(3)	(4)	(5)
50X.	Strengthening the curriculum	(1)	(2)	(3)	(4)	(5)
50Y.	Maintaining a high quality faculty	(1)	(2)	(3)	(4)	(5)
50Z.	Maintaining the physical plant	(1)	(2)	(3)	(4)	(5)
50AA.	Addressing issues of training for senior faculty	(1)	(2)	(3)	(4)	(5)
50BB.	Using quality management techniques (e.g. TQM)	(1)	(2)	(3)	(4)	(5)
50CC.	Addressing accountability issues	(1)	(2)	(3)	(4)	(5)
50DD.	Serving at-risk students	(1)	(2)	(3)	(4)	(5)
50EE.	Developing efficient advisory and registration systems and procedures	(1)	(2)	(3)	(4)	(5)
50FF.	Employing new teaching techniques	(1)	(2)	(3)	(4)	(5)

To what extent do you agree that the following are challenges you will have to face in your unit in the next **five years**:

		Strongly Agree	Agree	Neutral	Disagree	Strongly Disagree
50GG.	Identifying unit leadership potential from among the faculty	(1)	(2)	(3)	(4)	(5)
50HH.	Providing leadership training for faculty and chairs	(1)	(2)	(3)	(4)	(5)
50II.	Increasing emphasis on the transfer program	(1)	(2)	(3)	(4)	(5)
50JJ.	Utilizing more faculty development techniques such as classroom assessment, peer coaching, etc.	(1)	(2)	(3)	(4)	(5)

(Continued on next page)

Strategies

Below are listed several strategies useful in addressing the **challenges** (identified in Question 50). Indicate the extent to which you agree that the strategies would be useful to you in your current position:

		Strongly Agree	Agree	Neutral	Disagree	Strongly Disagree
51A.	Increasing the emphasis on long-range institutional planning	(1)	(2)	(3)	(4)	(5)
51B.	Developing unit mission statements	(1)	(2)	(3)	(4)	(5)
51C.	Developing campus-wide mission statements	(1)	(2)	(3)	(4)	(5)
51D.	Conducting internal/external environment assessments	(1)	(2)	(3)	(4)	(5)
51E.	Assessing future employment trends and opportunities	(1)	(2)	(3)	(4)	(5)
51F.	Conducting curriculum reviews to maintain relevance	(1)	(2)	(3)	(4)	(5)
51G.	Considering different approaches for allocating financial resources	(1)	(2)	(3)	(4)	(5)
51H.	Seeking external funding	(1)	(2)	(3)	(4)	(5)
51I.	Assessing leadership styles and profiles of the chairs	(1)	(2)	(3)	(4)	(5)
51J.	Writing job descriptions for chairs	(1)	(2)	(3)	(4)	(5)

161

Cont'd	Strategies

Below are listed several strategies useful in addressing the **challenges** (identified in Question 50). Indicate the extent to which you agree that the strategies would be useful to you in your current position:

		Strongly Agree	Agree	Neutral	Disagree	Strongly Disagree
51K.	Participating in training academy for chairs	(1)	(2)	(3)	(4)	(5)
51L.	Participating in regional conferences for chairs	(1)	(2)	(3)	(4)	(5)
51M.	Participating in national conferences for chairs	(1)	(2)	(3)	(4)	(5)
51N.	Participating in formal graduate courses	(1)	(2)	(3)	(4)	(5)
51O.	Reviewing and revising the organizational chart	(1)	(2)	(3)	(4)	(5)
51P.	Providing training for clerical and service personnel	(1)	(2)	(3)	(4)	(5)
51Q.	Clarifying roles and responsibilities of chairs	(1)	(2)	(3)	(4)	(5)
51R.	Assessing the professional development needs of chairs	(1)	(2)	(3)	(4)	(5)
51S.	Building stronger partnerships with business and industry	(1)	(2)	(3)	(4)	(5)
51T.	Emphasizing the integration of unit plans with institutional plans	(1)	(2)	(3)	(4)	(5)

Cont'd	Strategies

Below are listed several strategies useful in addressing the **challenges** (identified in Question 50). Indicate the extent to which you agree that the strategies would be useful to you in your current position:

		Strongly Agree	Agree	Neutral	Disagree	Strongly Disagree
51U.	Increasing staff development programs	(1)	(2)	(3)	(4)	(5)
51V.	Becoming involved in mentoring	(1)	(2)	(3)	(4)	(5)
51W.	Balancing personal and professional activities	(1)	(2)	(3)	(4)	(5)
51X.	Networking with other chairs	(1)	(2)	(3)	(4)	(5)

52. Do you want a brief summary of the study? (A report of this international study will be made at the 2nd International Conference of Community College Chairs and Deans, February 17-20, 1993, in Phoenix, Arizona.)
   (1)   Yes_____
   (2)   No_____

Thank you for completing this survey. Please return <u>only</u> your **machine-scorable response form**. Send it to the National Community College Chair Academy by **October 31, 1992** in the enclosed self-addressed envelope. If you have any questions, please contact: Gary L. Filan, Executive Director, National Community College Chair Academy, 1833 W. Southern Avenue, Mesa, Arizona 85202. Telephone: **(602)461-7304**

Plan to attend the 2nd Annual International Conference for Community College Chairs and Deans, Phoenix, Arizona, February 17-20, 1993. For information and registration call **(602)461-7304**

Appendix B

Research Procedures

Data Analysis Procedures

Data analyses for this project were completed utilizing the Statistical Package for the Social Sciences (SPSSx). This statistical software package allows for the analysis of very large data sets, and the management of complex analyses with speed and accuracy (Hinkle et al., 1988).

Descriptive Statistics

Early analyses focused on standard descriptive statistics. Each of the chapters include a table illustrating response frequencies, means and standard deviation for all survey questions.

Chapters presenting demographic information (two and three) include tables listing survey items in the order that they appeared on the instrument. Response options to these items were categorical, so in some cases averages represented a response range. In cases in which response categories were oppositional (e.g., gender) averages were not provided.

Chapters Four through Nine describe job dimensions; each include a table showing survey items. These are listed in rank order of the importance or agreement measured in terms of an average score on a 1-5 point Likert scale, ascribed to them by respondents.

Factor Analysis

Due to the bulk of survey items in each of the job dimensions sections of the survey (142 items in all) a factor analysis was performed. This research tool is utilized to determine if variations in the data can be "accounted for adequately by a number of basic categories smaller than that with which the investigation was started" (Fruchter, 1954, p. 1). In a sense, it allows the researcher to identify (exploratory) or create (confirmatory) clusters of items to use in further analysis (Crocker & Algina, 1986).

Initially, an exploratory factor analysis was completed. This process allowed the computer to generate categories based on responses, rather than relying on researcher hypotheses for the creation of categories. The SPSSx Factor Analysis program generated a multitude of potential factors, 28 of which showed statistical significance. Only factors (clusters) resulting in alpha levels greater than .5500 were included in further analysis; however, most of the clusters showed alpha levels of .7000 or greater.

Most of the generated clusters consisted of items that were in some way related, and could be analyzed and labeled appropriately. In a few cases, existing theoretical stances caused the researchers to manipulate individual items between clusters. Items were excluded from one factor and included in another only when such movement did not significantly detract from the reliability of either factor.

Each of the job dimension chapters includes a table and brief discussion of the clusters generated. Statistical tables showing correlations and alpha levels for each cluster are included as Appendix C.

Cross-tabulations

Once significant clusters had been identified, an analysis program was written to create the 28 new variables. All Likert scale response scores for each of the items within a cluster were added using a computer statement, and a new frequency distribution was run. Quartile scores 1-4 were then generated. For example, while a response to an individual item included in the Educational Beliefs and Values section could range from 1 (Strongly Agree) to 5 (Strongly Disagree), responses to the Beliefs clusters could only range from 1 (Agreement) to 4 (Disagreement).

The 28 cluster variables were then analyzed for variation in responses across 16 selected demographic characteristics (see discussion, Chapter Ten) using the SPSSx Crosstabs procedure. This resulted in 448 tables for examination, 247 of which showed significance at the .05 alpha level, and 187 which were significant at .00 alpha. Researchers then narrowed the list of crosstabs to include in their discussion to 121. These were products of comparisons between the seven demographic characteristics that influenced the most categories, which also showed .00 alpha significance. All 121 individual crosstab tables could not be included with this text; however, a compilation matrix showing the demographics, categories, and their significance levels is included as Table 10.1.

A few additional relational analyses were performed as ad hoc procedures, where it was determined that clarification of findings was needed. Results of these crosstabs are included in Chapter Two.

Appendix C

Factor Analysis Tables

Table C.1: Varimax Factor Analysis of Educational Beliefs and Values

Beliefs	Factor 1	Factor 2
Beliefs About Curriculum and Students		
Values education incorporated into the curriculum	.39717	
Opportunities for students to experience and understand leadership	.50881	
Using computers in the classroom	.37351	
Preparing students to meet the needs of the community	.55217	
Encouraging faculty to use a wide variety of teaching approaches	.54960	
Promoting and encouraging the enrollment of minority students in the college	.59793	
The concept of life-long learning	.44637	
Student support services	.61080	
Serving at-risk students	.67917	
Offering courses for limited English-speaking students	.58196	
Providing development courses to students	.57380	
Alpha	**.7798**	
Beliefs About Mission and Access		
Occupational/technical education		.50209
An open admission policy for my department (reverse code)		.56735
An open admission policy for my college (reverse code)		.51307
Preparing students to meet the needs of business/industry		.51794
Having selective admissions policies		.61477
The role of an advisory committee in establishing the curriculum		.35418
Alpha		**.5890**

Table C.2: Varimax Factor Analysis of Roles

ROLES	Factor 1	Factor 2	Factor 3
Interpersonal Role			
Information disseminator	.62838		
Facilitator	.47578		
Mentor	.46561		
Advocate	.56525		
Caretaker	.51176		
Alpha	**.5781**		
Administrator Role			
Resource allocator		.42560	
Evaluator		.57108	
Negotiator		.80872	
Conflict resolver		.76712	
Alpha		**.7076**	
Leader Role			
Visionary			.82413
Motivator			.68251
Entrepreneur			.49589
Delegator			.23082
Planner			.41693
Alpha			**.6187**

Table C.3: Varimax Factor Analysis of Tasks

TASKS	Factor 1	Factor 2	Factor 3
Professional Development and Communication Tasks			
Create a positive work environment	.51553		
Communicate needs to upper-level administrators	.50230		
Set personal and professional goals	.59901		
Encourage the professional development of each faculty member	.66153		
Promote affirmative action	.56957		
Communicate information from administration to unit faculty	.60800		
Alpha	**.7156**		
Faculty Selection & Feedback Tasks			
Recruit and select faculty		.68206	
Assign faculty responsibilities		.70673	
Evaluate faculty performance		.72117	
Provide feedback to faculty		.57460	
Terminate faculty		.64289	
Alpha		**.7766**	
Budget Tasks			
Prepare unit budgets			.80973
Monitor unit budgets			.81535
Allocate resources to priority activities			.69564
Alpha			**.8483**

Table C.3: Varimax Factor Analysis of Tasks (Cont'd)

TASKS	Factor 4	Factor 5	Factor 6	Factor 7
Internal Tasks				
Supervise clerical/technical staff	.76719			
Maintain unit data bases	.60530			
Manage facilities and equipment	.50256			
Develop clerical/technical staff	.73419			
Prepare enrollment projections	.37301			
Process paperwork and answer correspondence	.28352			
Alpha	**.7690**			
External Tasks				
Recruit students		.62324		
Develop relationships with business and community groups		.70497		
Seek external funding		.60835		
Alpha		**.6899**		
Curriculum and Student Tasks				
Schedule classes			.58001	
Update curriculum and courses			.54162	
Advise and counsel students			.70652	
Help students register			.66660	
Alpha			**.6021**	
Planning Tasks				
Integrate unit plans with institutional plans				.24755
Conduct unit meetings				.76547
Create unit committees				.74330
Develop long-range unit plans				.42470
Prepare for accreditation				.43999
Alpha				**.6791**

Table C.4: Varimax Factor Analysis of Skills

SKILLS	Factor 1	Factor 2	Factor 3
Administrative Skills and Leadership			
Problem analysis: Ability to seek out data and information to solve a problem	.73967		
Judgment: Ability to reach logical conclusions and make high quality decisions	.77642		
Organizational ability: Ability to be organized in dealing with a volume of paperwork and heavy demands on one's time	.54097		
Decisiveness: Ability to recognize when a decision is required	.68774		
Leadership: Ability to recognize when a group requires direction	.64111		
Alpha	**.7876**		
Interpersonal Skills			
Sensitivity: Ability to deal effectively with people		.55017	
Stress tolerance: Ability to perform under pressure		.65259	
Oral communication: Ability to make a clear oral presentation		.77603	
Written communication: Ability to express ideas clearly in writing		.78437	
Alpha		**.7439**	
Individual Skills			
Range of interests: Ability to discuss a variety of societal issues			.77338
Personal motivation: Ability to show a need to achieve			.83756
Educational values: Ability to be receptive to new ideas and change			.53588
Alpha			**.6636**

Table C.5: Varimax Factor Analysis of Job Challenges

CHALLENGES	Factor 1	Factor 2	Factor 3	Factor 4
Faculty Challenges				
Addressing issues of training for senior faculty	.57855			
Employing new teaching techniques	.44426			
Identifying unit leadership potential from among the faculty	.67156			
Providing leadership training for faculty and chairs	.71332			
Utilizing more faculty development techniques such as classroom assessment, peer coaching, etc.	.61938			
Alpha	**.7799**			
Student Challenges				
Offering courses through distance education		.41772		
Promoting greater gender equity		.55337		
Accommodating cultural diversity		.72743		
Responding to the needs of a wider range of students		.65395		
Serving at-risk students		.66849		
Attracting new student populations		.32994		
Alpha		**.7310**		
External Relations Challenges				
Decreasing growth in transfer programs			.56969	
Encouraging more technical preparation in high schools			.51950	
Increasing the use of business and industry advisory committees			.60970	

Table C.5: Varimax Factor Analysis of Job Challenges (Cont'd)

CHALLENGES	Factor 1	Factor 2	Factor 3	Factor 4
Increasing teaching programs sponsored by specific companies			.66298	
Adapting to employees who utilize electronic communication systems and who work at home			.53991	
Alpha			**.6818**	
Technology Challenges				
Changing the curriculum in response to technological development				.67161
Keeping pace with the increasing cost of technology				.71538
Securing and maintaining state-of-the-art technical equipment				.65036
Increasing the use of computers in classroom				.59496
Alpha				**.7127**

172

Table C.5: Varimax Factor Analysis of Job Challenges (Cont'd)

CHALLENGES	Factor 5	Factor 6	Factor 7	Factor 8	Factor 9
Program Quality Challenges					
Maintaining program quality	.80051				
Strengthening the curriculum	.78589				
Maintaining a high quality faculty	.72374				
Alpha	**.7957**				
External Accountability Challenges					
Increasing influence and impact of state coordinating bodies		.83000			
Increasing influence and impact of accrediting bodies		.82814			
Increasing involvement of the U.S. Government in establishing work conditions in colleges		.41366			
Alpha		**.7117**			
Financial Resources Challenges					
Obtaining financial resources			.68712		
Maintaining the physical plant			.68017		
Reallocating monies to programs because of financial constraints			.52665		
Alpha			**.5629**		

Table C.5: Varimax Factor Analysis of Job Challenges (Cont'd)

CHALLENGES	Factor 5	Factor 6	Factor 7	Factor 8	Factor 9
Curriculum Challenges					
Increasing general education requirements				.76866	
Increasing human relations training				.49584	
Internationalizing the curriculum				.44873	
Increasing emphasis on the transfer program				.43402	
Alpha				**.5837**	
International Accountability Challenges					
Using quality management techniques (e.g., TQM)					.42676
Addressing accountability issues					.43091
Developing efficient advisory and registration systems and procedures					.44468
Alpha					**.5779**

Table C.6: Varimax Factor Analysis of Strategies

STRATEGIES	Factor 1	Factor 2	Factor 3	Factor 4
Chair Development Strategies				
Assessing leadership styles and profiles of chairs	.64055			
Writing job descriptions for chairs	.68393			
Participating in a training academy for chairs	.80475			
Participating in regional conferences for chairs	.79242			
Participating in a national conference for chairs	.76376			
Participating in formal graduate courses	.42722			
Reviewing and revising the organizational chart	.53827			
Providing training for clerical and service personnel	.44386			
Clarifying roles and responsibilities of chairs	.66292			
Assessing the professional development needs of chairs	.63900			
Networking with other chairs	.47228			
Alpha	**.8949**			
Planning Strategies				
Increasing the emphasis on long-range institutional planning		.69917		
Developing unit mission statements		.81309		
Developing campus-wide mission statements		.82709		
Conducting internal/external assessments		.59173		
Emphasizing the integration of unit plans with institutional plans		.48372		

Table C.6: Varimax Factor Analysis of Strategies (Cont'd)

STRATEGIES	Factor 1	Factor 2	Factor 3	Factor 4
Conducting curriculum reviews to maintain relevance		.23165		
Alpha		**.8324**		
Personal & Professional Development Strategies				
Increasing staff development programs			.46825	
Becoming involved in mentoring			.48573	
Balancing personal & professional activities			.61190	
Alpha			**.6432**	
External and Financial Strategies				
Assessing future employment trends and opportunities				.58506
Considering different approaches for allocating financial resources				.64114
Seeking external funding				.75243
Building stronger partnerships with business and industry				.65240
Alpha				**.7262**